Saltwater Tales

D1608445

Offshore, Bay, and Surf Fishing Adventures
with Proven Tips and Techniques for the Saltwater Angler!

JOHN UNKART

Schiffer Publishing Ltd

4880 Lower Valley Road • Atglen, PA 19310

Another Title by John Unkart:
Offshore Pursuit: A Complete Guide to Blue-water Sport Fishing
ISBN: 978-0-7643-4308-7

Designed by RoS
Type set in Affair/Serifa BT

ISBN: 978-0-7643-4902-7
Printed in China

Published by Schiffer Publishing, Ltd.
4880 Lower Valley Road
Atglen, PA 19310
Phone: (610) 593-1777
Fax: (610) 593-2002
E-mail: Info@schifferbooks.com

For our complete selection of fine books on this and related subjects, please visit our website at www.schifferbooks.com. You may also write for a free catalog.

This book may be purchased from the publisher. Please try your bookstore first

We are always looking for people to write books on new and related subjects. If you have an idea for a book, please contact us at proposals@schifferbooks.com.

Schiffer Publishing's titles are available at special discounts for bulk purchases for sales promotions or premiums. Special editions, including personalized covers, corporate imprints, and excerpts can be created in large quantities for special needs. For more information, contact the publisher.

Dedication

Saltwater Tales is dedicated to Lenny Rudow,
the "Ultimate Angler."

Many years ago Lenny offered me the opportunity
to write an article for *Boating Magazine*, where he was an editor.
That opportunity began a journalism career and friendship
for which I am extremely thankful.

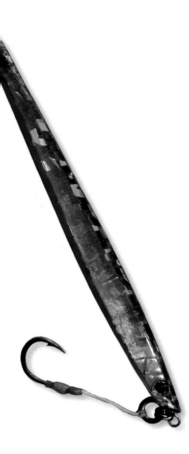

Introduction ... 7

Chapter 1: **Fall Flounder ... 8**
Rigging techniques with bait suggestions to catch doormat flounder

Chapter 2: **Mako Fishing ... 13**
Proven practices for catching mako sharks

Chapter 3: **Expectations! ... 20**
Trolling for yellowfin and deep dropping for golden tilefish

Chapter 4: **Revenge! ... 28**
Impaled by a white marlin

Chapter 5: **The Bite ... 32**
Trolling for yellowfin

Chapter 6: **Beast of the Beach ... 39**
Beach shark fishing technique

Chapter 7: **Should Have Been Here Yesterday! ... 46**
Charter boat chunkin techniques for tuna

Chapter 8: **White Marlin ... 52**
How to rig ballyhoo on circle hooks and using dredges

Chapter 9: **Just Never Know ... 58**
Offshore adventures that ended in catching fish unexpectedly

Chapter 10: **Spring Rock ... 65**
How to troll for striped bass with planer boards

Chapter 11: **Billfish Tournament Tactics ... 71**
Technique strategy when participating in billfish tournaments

Chapter 12: **Listen! ... 76**
Tips to prevent line separation

Chapter 13: **Bluefin ... 80**
Drift chunkin for bluefin

Chapter 14: **Balls of Fun ... 86**
Technique for bailing mahi mahi off lobster balls

Chapter 15: **Ocean Stripers ... 92**
Trolling for striped bass in fall/winter

Chapter 16: **Winter ... 96**
Fishing and physics

Chapter 17: **Toggin' Around ... 99**
Advice for catching tautog

Chapter 18: **Nature's Perfection ... 104**
Awe-inspiring moments found on the ocean

Chapter 19: **Trolling for *Coryphaena hippurus* ... 109**
Techniques and tips for catching mahi mahi

Chapter 20: **Nine No No's ... 114**
Mistakes no angler wants to make!

Chapter 21: **Wahoo ... 117**
Trolling methods that put wahoo in the killbox

Contents

Chapter 22: **Can I Die? ... 122**
Understanding seasickness

Chapter 23: **X Chromosome ... 124**
Females and fishing

Chapter 24: **Burn a Hole ... 126**
Charter boat trolling technique

Chapter 25: **Bluefin Strategies ... 130**
Understanding bluefin behavior to increase hookups

Chapter 26: **Three Fingers ... 135**
Old fisherman trick to increase catches

Chapter 27: **Fun in the Sun ... 137**
Fishing the barrier island of Assateague and Chincoteague

Chapter 28: **Ship-Shape Structure ... 146**
Making use of structure when fishing offshore

Chapter 29: **Sharks, Camera, Action! ... 148**
Catch and release tournament shark fishing

Chapter 30: **Chesapeake Chronicle ... 151**
History of Chesapeake Bay trolling

Chapter 31: **Black Gold ... 156**
Sea bass bottom fishing tips

Chapter 32: **Big Dog ... 162**
Catching a blue marlin

Chapter 33: **Getting Wet! ... 169**
Thoughts on the wisdom of backing down on fish

Chapter 34: **Tips & Tricks of the Trade ... 172**
Making life easier for the offshore angler

Chapter 35: **Captain Bligh ... 177**
Typical day of offshore charter fishing!

Chapter 36: **Don't Think! ... 181**
Turning bites into hooked up fish

Chapter 37: **Fly a Kite ... 184**
The art of fishing with a kite

Chapter 38: **Fishing Rough Water ... 188**
Is it worth the effort?

Chapter 39: **BFF Club ... 191**
Bottom fishing with friends and family

Chapter 40: **Going Deep in the Deep ... 196**
Deep dropping for golden tilefish

Chapter 41: **Best Job? ... 204**
Charter boat industry as a career

Chapter 42: **Catching Smiles! ... 207**

Acknowledgments ... 208

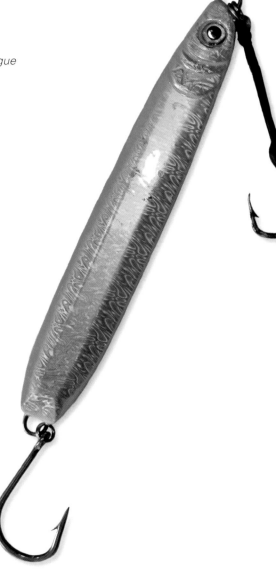

John Unkart has been relied upon for years to keep readers informed about cutting-edge tips and tactics to help us catch more fish. The barbed steel met the jaw in the straight how-to Offshore Pursuit, but here, in the highly entertaining pages of Saltwater Tales, the humor and anecdotal fun is cranked up like a pair of twin diesels headed to the edge. The steady pace of great fishing information and outlandish experiences provides a refreshing breeze as we embark on rod-bending, drag-screaming adventures.

—**Chris Lido**
Editor, New Jersey/Delaware Bay Edition
The Fisherman Magazine

John Unkart has managed to do what so many outdoors writers attempt, but fail to accomplish: he's combined entertaining storytelling with solid, valuable fishing knowledge. Each chapter is a pleasure to read, yet it's seeded with tips, tricks, and information that will help everyone become a better fisherman, from the beginner to the seasoned angler. Read this book for enjoyment; catch more fish as a much appreciated side effect.

—**Lenny Rudow**
Marine Editorial Services
Editor, Boats.com

Introduction

The author has wetted lines in the saltwater environment for over fifty years.

From angling for enjoyment on the Chesapeake Bay to chartering for a living in the canyons of the mid-Atlantic, he has spent a lifetime learning how to catch fish. This education was first shared in the how-to book *Offshore Pursuit.* Now, the author has penned *Saltwater Tales* and brings readers along on true-life fishing adventures where catch techniques are interwoven throughout the stories.

These chronicles are written as they unfolded, with many of the photos actually capturing moments of the catch. Readers will hopefully find the following pages an enjoyable read, while adding to their fishing knowledge—although, like the catch of a trophy fish that grows over time, there is the likelihood of an "exaggerated" truth here and there! However, the author attempted to stay away from the old adage, "Are all fisherman liars or do only liars fish?"

Chapter 1
Fall Flounder

Rigging techniques with bait suggestions to catch doormat flounder

Year after year, she was mysteriously drawn to an inlet cutting through a barrier island. Here, the vast water of the Atlantic Ocean flowed, mixing with bay water warmed under the sun of spring. After wintering and spawning on the edge of the mid-Atlantic continental shelf, as she had for the past ten years, an inner urge to move started her swimming westward on this year's voyage. Day after day, powerful tail thrust propelled her forward—light from above growing brighter as inshore shoals were approached. Occasionally, she lingered in a particular area for a day or two, feeding off the abundant schools of sand eels or squid before continuing the long journey. Finally, she arrived at a large cluster of rocks rising from the sea floor; she liked this area where water rushed down the rocky slope from thirty feet above. A buffet of food choices became caught up in violent, swirling currents caused by the rocks, creating easy meals. She felt comfortable in the bottom of this deep hole and took up temporary residence next to the large granite stones man used to create a jetty.

Over the next couple weeks, she feasted on appetizing morsels provided during tide changes every six hours. Finally, restlessness urged her once again to move on and it was only then she swam through the inlet created from a hurricane more than seventy years earlier. The violent storm left a forty mile-long barrier island shared by the states of Maryland and Virginia, where ancestors of horses from the seventeenth century still ran wild. Once in the bay, she turned southward and swam along the island's shoreline until coming upon a drop off in the bay floor. At the base of the slope, she buried herself with only eyes peering out of the sand and waited upon the next meal to ambush.

Over the next couple months, time passed while feasting on silversides, crabs, and small spot, washed out of marshes during outgoing tides. There had been no urgency to return to the dark, cold, offshore waters of the deep ocean. However, over summer, approximately four million eggs had developed in her stomach. And now, as bay water cooled with the onset of fall, she instinctively felt the need to move offshore and spawn once again. She moved along with hundreds of other flounder towards the inlet, carpeting the bay bottom like a moving rug. Mullet had invaded the bay a few weeks earlier, a favorite meal. She momentarily rested in a slight depression on the sandy bottom, waiting for one more of the tasty treats to come by to satisfy her appetite before moving on.

"No, missed them!" the Fisherman shouted over the sound of the engine, answering a question from the other man sitting behind the boat's helm. His voice had a tone of disgust, as the empty cast net was pulled from the water while he was trying to keep balance on the raised bow platform rocking back and forth. The net was reloaded on his arm, ready for another throw. Mullet are quick; a cast net must be thrown towards the front of a moving school if success is to be found. There was a time when throwing a heavy, ten-foot net with half-inch mesh that opened to a diameter of twenty feet was performed effortlessly. But years of hard work had taken its toll and arthritis now made throwing more difficult each fishing season. A lighter, six-foot net with ⅜" mesh was stored in a bucket on deck and easier to throw, but ⅜" mesh, while good for catching spot, did not fall quick enough to capture the speedy mullet that were often able to swim out from underneath before closing.

Another school of mullet was sighted creating rippled surface water along the edge of the marsh. The boat stealthy moved forward in their direction so not to frighten and drive the school deep. This time, the cast net opened perfectly, falling right on top the fleeing mullet.

"Got'em!"

As the mullet were gently being placed in a live well, the boat was already up on plane heading south behind Assateague Island.

"Where you want to start drifting this morning?"

"Let's try the west side where that cut dumps into the channel."

The two men knew the sand bars, drop offs, and location of bottom structure as well as anyone who fished the back bays. They were cousins, but more so best friends who had fished together over five decades and knew how to catch their fair share of the delicious, eating flounder. Many years ago, as kids, they figured out that anytime water flowed from a cut or lagoon into a channel on outgoing tide, fish normally gathered at the mouth to feast on the delicacies washed out. Flounder were no exception.

It was early fall; the tuna and marlin tournaments were over. Tourists were back at work in the big cities, leaving summer vacations at Ocean City, Maryland, only a memory. The bays were once again at peace; it was time to enjoy the pleasures of flounder fishing before bow hunting for deer began. Not to mention, frozen flounder filets in the freezer would make a nice addition for upcoming winter meals of surf and turf when sleet pelted the windows.

Flounder had spent summer spread out all over the back bays in small holes and channel cuts hiding from summer's boat activity and fishermen's hooks. But now, as water temperature dropped into the sixties, flounder congregated near the inlet to fill their stomachs on baitfish leaving the bay as well. Feeding heavily and gaining weight would be important if the flounder were to sustain the rigors of spawning and lean months ahead while wintering in the cold depths offshore.

"What kind of rig you got there?"

"A 4/0 wide gap gold hook with white mylar skirt. Tied up four dozen rigs on days charters got blown out. Tried something new and added red beads and gold spinner blades; looks good, huh? Not sure why, but flounder sure are partial to the color gold."

As the Fisherman was speaking, he netted a six-inch mullet from the live well and inserted the hook in only the upper part of the mouth. If the hook went through both the lower and upper parts of the mouth, the mullet would not be able to breathe and would not stay lively long.

The other angler hooked his mullet the same way on his old-type rig and noted while holding it up to be admired, "Your new rig sure is pretty with beads and all, but a plain gold hook is all that we've ever needed to catch a flounder!"

They nodded in agreement as smiles developed. It had always been in the Fisherman's nature to try and find new ways to catch fish, even though old methods were proven to work. Both men were using a fish-finder rig. This allowed the flounder to inhale bait without feeling the weight of the sinker. Hooks were snelled on thirty-inch-leaders with a barrel swivel at the other end for line attachment. This allowed the bait to trail a couple feet behind the sinker.

The overcast morning with calm wind and clear clean water combined to make conditions perfect for flounder fishing. The boat would not present much of a shadow as it drifted along effortlessly in the shallow water—certainly an advantage. It was prime time of the year for catching a prized "doormat," the term used for flounder weighing more than five pounds. Compared to the hordes of vacationers who rented Jet Skis and wreaked havoc for anglers during summer months, the one Jet Ski that occasionally buzzed by was hardly noticed. Conversations mostly centered on reminiscing about summer catches, interrupted occasionally by a flounder that found one of their mullet appealing. When this occurred, the rod tip would be lowered slightly so the fish had slack to swallow the bait before the hook was set. After years of practice, seldom did either of the men miss hooking a fish. After the flounder was netted and placed on ice in the cooler, conversation would continue.

The Fisherman charter fished, making a living by taking tourists offshore to catch fish most anglers only dreamt about. It had been a busy charter season, the first year in many that a good chunk bite developed for yellowfin and bluefin tuna on the inner lumps between the twenty- and thirty-fathom lines. And there were trips well offshore to the canyons, where beautiful, colored mahi had been caught under poly buoys attached to lobster pots laying on the ocean floor below in 600 feet of water. White marlin sparkled rainbow colors in sunlight after feeling a circle hook in the corner of the mouth, causing acrobatic jumps several feet in the air. Many trips targeted sea bass, blueline, or golden tilefish. But for now, one of the Fisherman's favorite pastimes had arrived: fall flounder fishing.

Fishing was a hobby for the Fisherman's cousin. He was a commercial crabber, spending days of summer under blistering sun, catching the delicious delicacy tourist craved, steamed with Old Bay seasoning and kosher salt. It had been a good summer of fishing and crabbing—as good as any in many a year—and stories flowed, as each remembered another detail as to why fish or crabs were caught on a particular day. Even though both men spent just about every day on the water, they looked forward to each other's company and the relaxation flounder fishing provided.

"Get ready; depth finder shows we are beginning to drop down the edge."

Both anglers opened the bails on their spinning reels, allowing sinkers to maintain contact with the bottom as water became deeper.

The flounder was lying in a twelve-foot depression. A puff of sand on the bottom followed by a flash caught its attention. A struggling mullet slipped by, triggering the feeding instinct. She bolted out from under the sand and, with a couple flips of the tail, caught up to the shiny, flashing meal. The large mouth, full of teeth, opened, engulfing the mullet in one swift bite before swimming back towards her ambush spot.

Often, flounder require two bites to get down big bait like the Fisherman had on his hook. But the six-inch mullet was an easy swallow for this fish.

Normally, the Fisherman would count to three after a bite, allowing the bait to be swallowed before setting the hook. But there was no tell-tail sign that a bite was occurring. It surprised him when the rod almost jerked out of his hand. It bent over double and drag started singing.

"Got a nice bluefish or trout?"

"No, I can feel a head shake; it's definitely a flounder!"

Hook inserted through only the upper part of the mouth allows mullet to live until it becomes a meal!

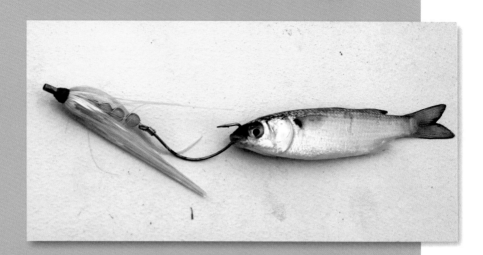

Flounder-Pounder rigs can be purchased, but are easily constructed; components are available at most tackle shops, so anglers can create their own killer rigs like the Fisherman's.

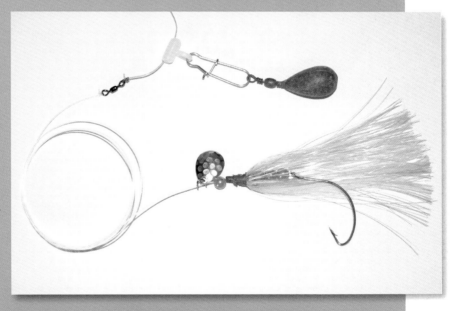

The flounder made it down to the safety of bottom, only to abruptly find itself heading towards the surface again. A strange feeling was coming from the corner of its mouth—no pain, but whatever was there could not be dislodged with violent head-shakes. Time after time she swam for the bottom with powerful tail strokes, until every last bit of energy was expelled. Light from above became brighter.

The net was already in hand waiting to be used.
"Holy #%@, look at this one; don't miss it!"
Since a flounder cannot swim backwards, the net was dipped from in front and swept towards the tail. This forces the flounder to swim into the net, reducing the chance of an escape. One quick dip motion and the flounder found itself in a strange environment. The fish formed a large-shaped "U" in the bottom of the net. The men grinned at one another, until finally the crabber spoke, "Damn nice fish; got an extra one of those gold hook spinner rigs?"

Tackled!

⚓ **THROWING A CAST NET**
⚓ **RIGGING MULLET**
⚓ **SOLID HOOK SETTING**

The Fisherman displays the flounder that will not be going back offshore to spawn and spend winter.

Chapter 2

Mako Fishing

Proven practices for catching mako sharks

The Fisherman was staring at sea temperature satellite shots on the computer screen, trying to decide where to go or what species to target the next day. Unconsciously, the old, tattered John Deere baseball cap was removed and scratching began on his balding head. The next day's crew would be buddies and an empty fish box was not an option or he would never hear the end of it. It was early summer and offshore the ocean was coming alive. A temperature shot showed an eddy of warm water had spun off the Gulf Stream and was drifting westward behind Washington Canyon. The next day might be the perfect opportunity to catch a few early-season yellowfin or mahi in the body of water. The eddy was just outside the 500-fathom line; it would be a long run. But a white marlin might even be there. Every year the Marlin Club and town of Ocean City, Maryland, teamed up to award $10,000 to whoever caught the first white marlin and, to date, none had been caught. Earlier in the week, a deep drop trip had produced a nice bunch of golden tilefish for clients. Good numbers of lean, mean bluefish were on all the inner lumps, a lot of fun to catch on light tackle. Of course, mako sharks migrating northward would be taking up temporary residence along the twenty-fathom line to dine on the bluefish, one of their favorite meals. The agonizing decision as to what species in the vast ocean to chase was made easier after the thought of mouth-watering mako steaks on the grill came to mind. Yep, it tipped the scale towards sharking. Well, that and a forecast of 15 knots SE wind which would make a seventy-five-mile run to the deep a very sloppy and uncomfortable ride. The crew was called and told to be at the boat by 5 a.m.; they were going after mako.

Mako (*Isurus oxyrhincus*) are the fastest swimming sharks and have been clocked close to thirty MPH in burst. This means a smoking reel when the hook finds its mark. Combine that with spectacular jumps two or three times in length and it is easy to see why mako are considered a sport fish by many anglers.

Next morning, engines fired up and the boat eased out of the slip at 5:15 a.m. The Fisherman hoped to get offshore before the morning breeze began to pick up. Rule of thumb: wind comes up with the sun. While there are exceptions, most days anglers will find that getting an early start often provides a decent run on gentle seas the first hour or so before wind begins to build seas. On this day, ten miles off the beach, morning greeted everyone with an ominous-looking sunrise. A wary eye would clearly be needed on the radar for a stray thunderstorm with the unstable air mass…this was not forecasted!

It was the Fisherman's intention to troll up a few bluefish at a local lump twenty-one miles from the inlet called the Jackspot. A couple blues would be kept alive in the live well. They would be bridle rigged and suspended under a kite as bait. A bluefish struggling on the surface is a hard bait to beat for a big ravenous mako. The rest would be placed on ice. Each side of the bluefish would be filleted and then cut into strip baits about a foot long and three or four inches wide. However, apparently the bluefish were not made aware of this plan. After two hours of trolling, there was nothing to show for the effort.

The Fisherman was somewhat disgusted. "Get the frozen mackerel out of the freezer and throw it in a bucket with saltwater to start thawing; crank in the lines."

The crew squared away the trolling gear as the boat came up on plane for a twelve-mile run to an edge where the Fisherman has caught many mako over the years. The location was the site of the *Marine Electric*, a 605-foot coal ship that made a routine run from Norfolk, Virginia, to Somerset, Massachusetts. However, on a trip off the coast of Virginia, on February 10, 1983, the ship was caught in a Nor'easter blow that produced twenty-five-foot waves. The old ship, built in 1944, went down to the bottom and now rested near a finger jutting out on the twenty-fathom line, where a depth of 128 feet rose up to ninety feet.

Normally, an edge like this produced good shark fishing. Add in a wreck, and it was a fish-attracting location. The Fisherman did not know if it was the upwelling created from the depth change or the old coal ship that sank to its death that attracted sharks to the area. But most of the time, sharks could be counted on to provide action at this location. Blue sharks, thresher, hammerhead, and mako all found this edge to their liking and had been caught at one time or another.

Fresh bait is always best when shark fishing; tuna bellies, bluefish, or false albacore filets on hooks draw a lot of shark attention. However, with no fresh bait, frozen mackerel would be counted on to entice a set of mako teeth to a hook, along with use of a chum bucket and menhaden oil dripping into the water. The Fisherman preferred Mackerel chum, but the tackle shop had run out and only had ground menhaden when picking up a couple buckets the evening before. It would suffice, but mackerel chum worked better in his opinion.

The GPS beeped, indicating the boat had arrived at the location. After watching the chart plotter for a couple minutes to obtain drift direction, the boat was positioned one-half mile above a slight depression on the ocean floor near the wreck. The chum bucket and drip bag were deployed along with three rods staggered at various depths. One rod suspended a mackerel just five feet under a float seventy-five yards behind the boat; this was called the surface bait rod. The bait on this rod hung right beneath the chum slick. Oil from chum stays on the surface and forms a slick, which, on a nice day can, draw sharks for a good distance. The suspended bait just underneath could almost always be counted on for a bite or two. Second rod suspended a mackerel thirty feet under a float forty yards behind the boat with a four-ounce sinker to prevent bait from rising in the current. The third rod had bait five cranks off the bottom with sixteen-ounce weight to keep the mackerel down. This rod was fished directly under the boat. The fourth rod, a kite rod, was always deployed when a breeze was present. Live bait swimming in circles on the surface can't be beat. But with lack of live bait this day, a thawed mackerel skirted in a red squid skirt was floating about on the surface until something could be cranked off bottom and rigged as live bait. Mako seemed partial to red skirts, but only in the top ten feet of water. If used below that depth, the light spectrum under water made the red skirt appear brown. A couple anglers had spinning gear in hand, bottom fishing with squid, while everyone else sat back to relax and discuss all the topics that come under the title:

Mako test the ability of anglers with aerial acrobatics and drag busting runs. Once a hook comes tight, it is truly a fight of man against beast.

While gray skies do not always mean storms, it is prudent to keep an eye on the radar and have rain gear handy on mornings like this with unstable air mass.

"What is said on the boat, stays on the boat!"

Fortunately, the crew was just scratching the surface of the first topic when the unmistakable *click-click-click* sound came from the rod with mackerel suspended under the float at five feet. The Fisherman picked up the rod and allowed line to peel off the spool with no pressure for a few seconds. Once he was sure the bait had been swallowed, the Penn International's drag screamed when the hook found the corner of the mouth. Three strong settings of the J-hook made sure it was driven home to stay. The rod was handed off to a buddy, who was already in a harness and fighting belt. The tug of war began.

Moments later, the shark skyrocketed ten feet out of the water; the crew yelled in unison "MAKO!" It performed a patented twirl and somersault, ending with a large explosion-type splash. At 100 yards from the boat, it was clear this shark would be killed for the dinner table if the opportunity presented itself.

Anglers should never count chickens before they are hatched, and hooking a mako and getting one tied off the side of the boat is like mixing apples and oranges. For those who may not have caught a mako, after deciding to boat the shark, controlled, mass confusion erupts. Knowing you'll be dealing with a dangerous set of teeth is enough to raise the "pay attention" bar. A team effort is required to land a decent-sized mako and everyone is given a task. Actually, the angler has the easy job: he/she only has to wind the shark to the boat! Someone needs to be at the controls of the boat to position it properly, depending on how the mako runs. The helmsman tries to keep the mako behind the transom during the battle. The chum bucket and fishing lines need to be cleared from the pit, giving room for whatever might occur—and "whatever" often does occur with mako. One note of caution: make sure the menhaden oil drip does not continue to drip inside the boat in the excitement of clearing lines and gear to fight the shark. This occurred once (only once!); it is impossible to stand up on an oil-covered deck, let alone fight a shark while doing so!

But getting back to duties, someone needs to gaff the mako; but first, someone has to wire the shark within gaffing distance. This can be the most dangerous task and often where a mako is lost. Never take more than one wrap around a hand when wiring a shark. If multiple wraps are taken and become tangled, the wireman could find him/herself pulled out of the boat. Finally, someone is responsible for getting a tail rope on the shark. This can be accomplished by placing a big loop around the tail of the mako, or around the head and sliding the loop down over the shark to the tail section where the loop is tightened. However, all sharks are not comfortable with this procedure! With all required tasks covered, the Fisherman prepared the flying gaff. When an opportunity was presented for a shot, the gaff was sunk and the mako went ballistic.

After a few touch-and-go moments, the tail rope was tight and the Mako was secured to the port side of the boat. As the ropes were tied off, the Fisherman told a story about how, years before, he only tail roped sharks and hung them from the tuna tower frame. The tail would be out of the water but the body remained in water while waiting for the shark to expire. On one occasion, two hours after being caught, a 150-pound mako decided it would rather be in the boat instead of out and flipped into the cockpit. Upon hitting the deck, the thrashing tail slipped out of the tail rope giving the shark full access to the cockpit. The snapping teeth vacated the pit real quick; anglers ended up in the cabin and standing outside the boat on the swim platform. Fortunately, none of the charter was injured. Since that time, sharks are now secured to two cleats. Rope from the flying gaff secures the head of the shark to a front cleat and tail rope secures to a rear cleat.

16

The National Oceanic and Atmospheric Administration (NOAA) regulations currently allow one mako shark per boat, with a minimum of a fifty-four-inch forked tail length. With the crew's retention allotment met, the lines were reset for some fun fishing and, over the next couple hours, three more sharks were caught and released—two dusky and one brown—but no more mako were hooked to put on an entertaining aerial show.

The weatherman was horribly mistaken this day with his forecast of 15 knot wind (like that never occurs!) and seas built throughout the day. On the thirty-three-mile trek back to port, wind was blowing twenty with gusts over twenty-five MPH. The Fisherman had made the right call this day staying close to shore. The crew was happy and didn't seem to mind spray as it flew over the boat.

As the boat fought its way back to port, the Fisherman thought how the 220-pound mako would provide many mouth-watering steaks for the crew. The aroma could almost be detected coming off the grill.

Mako Steaks

Serves four (½ pound per person)

Ingredients:
  4 mako filets
  ½ cup melted butter
  1 tablespoon fresh basil
  1 tablespoon garlic powder
  1 tablespoon parsley
  Pepper, to taste
  Salt, to taste
  Lemon juice, a splash

Directions:
This Fisherman's favorite recipe calls for melted butter mixed with fresh basil, garlic powder, and parsley. A few dashes of pepper and salt to taste and a splash of lemon juice are thrown in for good measure before mixing well. The mako filets are placed in the concoction for thirty minutes before finding their way to a hot grill and flipped over after three or four minutes. Be careful not to overcook the meat, as this ruins the flavor.

As the boat backed into its slip, someone quipped, "Hey, why didn't we catch any tuna today?"

The crew laughed at the question like it was the funniest thing they'd ever heard.

The Fisherman just shook his head and thought, *That first beer was going to taste real good!*

A flying gaff is essential for landing mako. Make sure gaff rope is tied off to a cleat; mako go ballistic when feeling the cold steel.

Tackled !

⚓ DETERMINING DRIFT
⚓ BAIT
⚓ CHUMMING
⚓ GAFFING AND LANDING

Landing a mako like this takes teamwork. Many mouth-watering
steaks for the grill hanging here.

Chapter 3
Expectations!

Trolling for yellowfin and deep dropping for golden tilefish

The Fisherman had been keeping eyes on the weather forecast, with ears on fishing reports from anglers trolling the Baltimore Canyon. For the previous week or so, the bite had been pretty consistent, with catches of yellowfin and bigeye tuna. The Fisherman did not have charters the previous couple days and had blocked out the next day as a family/friends' day on the ocean. The crew was counting on fresh sushi for Sunday dinner. The Fisherman always felt pressure to catch fish for clients, but when family or friends were on the boat, the pressure seemed to increase. A couple phone calls to charter captains in the evening confirmed the yellowfin bite was still going off in the Baltimore Canyon, but with many undersized throwbacks.

Up to date information is a key factor when it comes to being successful offshore. The ocean is a big place to search for fish. Anglers without charter or commercial connections might try obtaining recent-catch information on social media fishing sites for their area, such as in the mid-Atlantic, Tidalfish.com, SportsFisherman.com, or any one of the many local marinas posting fishing reports daily. While exact information might not be given, it at least gives anglers a general location to begin fishing and to search for what is biting. But the information must be taken with a grain of salt; after all, fishermen are posting the information!

Saturday morning, the crew was pumped with the Fisherman's catch report as they climbed aboard for the day. It was an early start and, by 4:30 a.m., the boat cleared the C-Buoy with GPS numbers punched in for a location just southeast of the Baltimore bight. The Fisherman did not have any idea of the total number boats that fished out of Ocean City, Maryland; Indian River, Delaware; and Cape May, New Jersey, but on this morning, the radar showed every one was converging with him at the Baltimore Canyon!

Tuna are sight feeders and a bright moon allows fish to feed all night. The moon draws baitfish to the surface, allowing predators looking up to easily see silhouettes of schooled baitfish. It is always best to plan fishing trips on the dark side of the moon, when possible. On this trip, a rare, super moon occurred the night before the trip, which would be sure to put a damper on the early morning bite. But anglers must fish when time/opportunity allows. To compensate for less-than-perfect fishing conditions, anglers often need to be flexible and willing to change tactics or targeted species in order to find success.

With several bigeye tuna caught the previous few days, a mixed spread for yellowfin and bigeye was set behind the transom to begin this day. This consisted of three spreader bars with nine-inch squid and five medium-sized ballyhoo skirted with Ilanders and Sea Witches. This created an eight-line spread of decent-

The first legal yellowfin this day fell for a Green Machine rigged behind a psycho-colored spreader bar. Replacing the last squid on spreader bar with a Green Machine is SOP in the charter industry.

sized bait to draw the attention of 200-pound bigeye, but still be appetizing to yellowfin. In the first hour, three small yellowfin found the ballyhoo baits to their liking; however, no tails reached the twenty-seven-inch minimum length on the rule and they were released to grow for another day.

Bigeye favor 100 fathoms or more water beneath them and seldom are caught shallower. So the boat worked into the deep and trolled the east and west walls of the canyon for the next couple hours in 200-500 fathoms of water. Literally hundreds of boats took advantage of the flat seas this day and were fishing the area, but none were observed hooked up. Finally, the Fisherman worked the boat back to where lines were first placed in the water. It was nearing noon before the first bent rod was observed on another boat. The noon bite had showed up! Over the next half hour, several fish were boated. The radio, mostly silent all morning, lit up with reports of bigeye hooked and several yellowfin caught.

For whatever reason, tuna seem to hang around whales and porpoises. When this type of life is observed in the deep, trolling the area hard often results in bites. A pod of pilot whales were found in seventy fathoms and the Fisherman crisscrossed the area several times until the first yellowfin over twenty-seven inches found its way into the killbox.

The tuna bite was less than stellar: three were in the killbox, but expectations were a lot greater. The Fisherman pointed the bow towards a tiny blip on the chart plotter forty-three miles to the south. It would be a long run, but the location had "always" produced fish. The boat trolled that direction for another hour before managing another doubleheader of yellowfin. Lines were then pulled and everyone settled in for the 1½-hour run.

Picking up lines and running to a bite after hearing radio fish caught is something the Fisherman did not often do—it seldom seemed to pay off in reward. By the time lines were back in the water at the new location, the bite was normally over. However, making this long run was different, since tactics were being changed from trolling to deep dropping for golden tilefish. Also, it was a proven location where the Fisherman always found luck, even when fish appeared to have lockjaw, on any particular day.

Torsa high-speed reels on Trevela rods were dug out of the cabin in exchange for the Penn International trolling outfits. When everyone was ready with rod in hand, the first drift was set up in 720 feet of water. It takes a couple minutes for the whole squid and clam baits to hit bottom when deep dropping; anglers not ready may miss the prime territory drift when orders are given to "let'em go!" Often, golden tilefish live in an area no larger than a football field. This may sound like a large area, but not in terms of being on the bottom of the ocean! It only took a few minutes of waiting, once bait hit bottom, for the first bent rod to double over, immediately followed by a second rod, then a third! After twenty minutes of cranking, a triple header of golden tilefish came over the gunwale.

On every deep dropping adventure, the Fisherman tried to find a new location to catch golden tilefish. He called this "prospecting" and, while not always successful, was certainly worth the effort when a new location was found. Golden tilefish are very slow growing and finding new locations to catch fish spreads out pressure; this prevents fishing out any one particular area. Tilefish form colonies and stay put—meaning, once you locate the fish, they will be there time after time, until the colony is depleted. This is why the Fisherman felt it important to have many fishing locations for them—to preserve both the species and good fishing. On any particular day, the Fisherman only allowed a handful of fish to be caught at any one location.

It is very common when drifting over prime area of a colony for multiple hookups of golden tilefish to occur. This triple header put smiles on everyone's faces!

As in this case, most golden tiles will be caught on the bottom hook. These fish are true bottom huggers.

The Fisherman's brother-in-law with a well-deserved catch, after a twenty-minute tug of war.

The blueline tilefish is found in shallower water than its larger cousin the golden tilefish, normally near the fifty-fathom line.

Sea bass can be found anywhere from back bays to offshore. But savvy anglers concentrate efforts in deeper water to catch "knotheads." Large sea bass are often found mixed in with blueline tilefish.

On this day, he let the boat drift after the triple header, instead of running back up for another drift over the colony. For the next forty minutes, the boat drifted a mile in 600-700 feet of water, prime depth for golden tile, before a rod again doubled over with a fish from a new, virgin colony. A grunt was let out by the Fisherman's brother-in-law as the golden tilefish, close to fifty pounds, attempted to swim back down to the safety of its burrow after swimming out to devour a squid. The golden tile gave a tough fight, but finally gave in to the pressure pulling him upwards. As sweat dripped off the brother-in-law's forehead, the fish finally broke the surface to be gaffed.

Another species often caught in the vicinity of golden tiles is black-belly rose fish, commonly known as red rosies. These delicious, eating fish are not very large, but greeted with enthusiasm after cranking in close to 1,000 feet of line. Similar in shape to a sea bass, they have large mouths capable of swallowing 11/0 circle hooks intended for the tilefish. These rosies were a welcome addition to the killbox.

A couple more golden tiles were gaffed and everyone agreed that enough were in the killbox. There is no releasing golden tilefish. They come to the surface with their air bladder inflated and often near death.

The clock showed there was still time to squeeze in an hour or so of some blueline tilefish and sea bass fishing. Both of these species are caught in shallower water. It would not be out of the way on the run home, so a short run in to the fifty-fathom line and the boat stopped over a honey hole that, for years, produced both species. Half the crew used jigs with hooks, sweetened with pieces of squid; the other half used standard two-hook bottom rigs with squid. As soon as lines hit bottom, rods bent over and several nice fish joined the other fish in the killbox.

After years of deep dropping, the Fisherman's records show jigs out-fish standard bottom rigs. Today was no different, with the largest sea bass and bluelines engulfing the jigs. A piece of squid on a jig hook seems to entice the larger fish. But a plain jig is all that's necessary when fish are hungry.

The lids on the killboxes finally got to the point where no more fish were going to be squeezed in. No one complained when the Fisherman called it a day and, with tired arms and big smiles, everything was squared away for the sixty-five-mile run back to port. A more beautiful day could not have been scripted on the ocean. The sun called it quits and said good night when the boat was still ten miles off the beach.

Once at the dock, and after off-loading 485 pounds of fish to be cleaned, the crew was in agreement...the day had exceeded everyone's expectations!

Tackled!

- ⚓ SETTING A TROLLING SPREAD
- ⚓ TROLLING PRIME AREA FOR YELLOWFIN AND BIGEYE
- ⚓ PREFERRED DEPTH FOR GOLDEN TILEFISH
- ⚓ PRESERVING THE TILEFISH FISHERY

The black belly red rose fish obtains its name from a black inner stomach liner. This species is delicious on a dinner plate.

Sunset closes the door on another day offshore.

Chapter 4

Revenge!

Impaled by a white marlin

There was an incredible white marlin bite going off one fall in the mid-Atlantic. Typical of migrating white marlin, the bite had begun in Wilmington Canyon off New Jersey and, over a couple weeks, moved south down into Norfolk Canyon off Virginia. The action was pretty steady every day and the charter fleet followed the bite. Releases of a dozen or more whites per boat each day was common with some boats in the twenties. The Fisherman was mating on one of the charter boats.

The charter's shouting was deafening as the white marlin made a spectacular jump thirty feet from the side of the boat. Using the last bit of energy for the final act of its performance, the exhausted fish turned on its side. The Fisherman joined in the crew's jubilation by shouting congratulations to the angler on catching his first white marlin, as the leader was grabbed and fish wired to the transom.

When billfishing, once the leader is touched by the mate, the fish is considered a legal catch by IGFA (International Game Fish Association). Normally, the fish is released at this point and not brought into the boat, but as the Fisherman leaned over the transom to remove the hook, he heard, "Can you bring it in the boat for a photo?"

Feeling obliged after the charter forked over a lot of hard-earned cash to fish offshore for the day—not to mention his payday would be the tip from the charter—he agreed and asked everyone to step back. Gloves protecting hands while wiring the fish were dipped in the ocean and made wet. The wetness helps avoid rubbing off protective slime, which is part of the fish's immune system. Carefully and gently, the fifty-pound white was lifted out of the water to prevent any injury. However, a quick flip of the tail while being pulled over the gunwale catapulted the fish skyward. Unfortunately, what goes up, must come down. Time seemed to stand still for the Fisherman as one hand's grip was lost and all he could do was watch as the bill embedded in his left thigh, despite all effort to avoid it. Fortunately, the bill missed the femur artery, leaving only a deep puncture wound in the muscle, which would later require medical attention at the hospital. A photo was quickly taken of the angler with his trophy before the fish was released to look for a more accommodating meal. The wound was bandaged and the day of fishing continued. The bruise and soreness of the tetanus shot given at the emergency room that night lasted a couple days. The humiliation is said to still exist today!

Impaling number two occurred to the Fisherman the following year (yes, lightning can strike twice) during the most prestigious billfish tournament in the world, the White Marlin Open, held out of Ocean City, Maryland, during the first

Anglers are seldom disappointed with the aerobatics of a white marlin.

The Fisherman indicates how the day is going after being impaled by a white marlin bill.

week of August. Not only is this the most prestigious billfish tournament to win, but it also pays out the most award money of all billfish tournaments.

The charter was in an uproar every time the marlin displayed shimmering rainbow colors in the bright sunlight while somersaulting out of the water during the battle. And when the Fisherman finally got his hands on the bill, the shouting erupted even louder. The white marlin was of good size and a possible contender. It would need to be brought onboard for measurement. If the tell of the tape measured a minimum of sixty-eight inches and fish weighed at least seventy pounds, there would be a trip to the tournament scale that could be worth well over a million dollars in prize money.

But once again, as the white was being boated, there was a quick flip of the tail and the fish was heading towards the heavens—talk about déjà vu! The whole event occurred in slow motion. The marlin momentarily hung in midair angled down towards the Fisherman's leg. Hands tightened their grip on the bill, but to no avail. The bill slipped through the wet gloves and the needle-sharp weapon disappeared into the *same* leg! With the crew's help, the bill was retracted, followed by pulsating squirts of blood. And to add insult to injury, the fish was an inch short and had to be released.

The Fisherman and captain assessed the injury and decided the injury could wait for medical attention. After all, this was the White Marlin Open Tournament! The leg was bandaged tightly; although bleeding slowed, it never stopped completely and the throbbing continued for the next two hours until, finally, 3:30 p.m. arrived and "lines out of water" came over the radio. It was a long ride back to port, even with the leg elevated. Somewhere around midnight in the emergency room, a few stitches finally stopped the bleeding. At least there was no need for a tetanus shot!

While dangers of fishing are not routinely thought about, they certainly exist. Hooks being removed while fish flop around on deck is a big culprit, not to mention bites from bluefish or other toothy critters. Billfish normally do not raise concern—but should, as previous incidents demonstrate. However, a billfish does not have to be brought onboard a boat to be dangerous.

The Fisherman was working a private sixty-two-footer for a well-to-do owner who only fished for white marlin. The Fisherman's responsibility this day was controlling two dredges and teasers, used to attract marlin into the spread behind the transom. These were controlled from the bridge; another mate had the duties of working lines in the pit with the owner. During what should have been a routine catch and release, a white marlin turned and charged the boat as it was backing down so the angler could gain line. Suddenly, the fish went airborne and narrowly missed impaling the mate.

While fish certainly do not understand revenge (well, let's hope not), at times, they seem to try to get back at anglers. Don't allow what should be a lifetime memory to become ruined by an unexpected incident. When fishing, always stay alert, keep your guard up, carry a big pair of side cutters for hooks that become impaled, stock a first-aid kit, and expect the unexpected!

Tackled!

⚓ **EXTREME CAUTION REQUIRED WHEN BILLFISHING**

Without warning, this white marlin turned and charged the boat while backing down.

White marlin can easily clear a transom.

The mate narrowly escaped serious injury from the deadly, pointy weapon just missing his body. After photos, the fish was released to "attack" another day!

Chapter 5

The Bite

Trolling for yellowfin

The school of yellowfin tuna moved in sync as one. Up, down, turning, and twisting: an aquatic ballet being performed underwater. Since birth, the school had been highly migratory and, for most of the first year, swam off the coast of South America, where they numbered in the tens of thousands—all carbon copies of one another. But nature can be cruel and, now, at two years of age, a length of thirty-six inches, and weight of about thirty-five pounds, the school's number had dwindled down to a few hundred. Blue marlin, wahoo, and other predators feasted upon the school when young. Recreational fishermen's hooks harvested many of the fish when migrating up the East Coast of the United States. However, commercial longlines and trawler nets were responsible for reducing the majority of the school.

Another school of much larger, four-year-old yellowfin had been moving northward as well, following the warming summer water, full of life, when a commercial net enclosed them. A few tuna managed to escape and, somewhere off the coast of South Carolina, one of these stragglers began following the smaller school for the past couple weeks. Being much larger, this tuna did not swim within the school, but felt comfortable just staying close. As dawn introduced another day to the world, the school found themselves off the coast of Virginia, swimming in a canyon known to anglers as The Norfolk.

Norfolk Canyon is one of fifteen canyons along the eastern United States—each cutting a trough into the continental shelf, formed a couple million years earlier by glaciers. The Norfolk is one of the largest canyons where depths exceed 9,800 feet. The change in water depth causes upwelling along the canyon walls, bringing cold, bottom water full of nutrients to the surface. Once sunlight hits the nutrients, algae explodes, beginning a food chain. The food chain ends with the top predator—anglers—catching fish.

It takes an enormous amount of food to sustain the energy to swim nonstop as tuna do. And the previous moonless night made feeding difficult.

Earlier in the evening, the school came upon squid swimming up out of the deep depths of the canyon. The fish drove the squid to the surface where, in the blackness of night, mayhem occurred. It happened quickly and, within a couple minutes, the squid had vanished into stomachs, and calmness to the ocean surface returned. But that was hours before and now it was time to feed once again.

As the sun crested the eastern horizon, it painted a crimson sky, as an artist would when putting a brush to canvas; the school was below on the prowl. Soft, morning light filtering down into the ocean allowed silhouettes of flying fish to be observed and several fish from the school streaked upwards, jumping out of the water chasing one of their favorite meals.

The charter had booked a tuna trip; the crew consisted of three couples in their mid-thirties. Although the men had chartered before, it was the first time for the two wives and girlfriend. The Fisherman was working as Mate this day. As the boat cleared the inlet in the wee hours of morning, everyone was in the cabin asking the Fisherman questions. The girls were apprehensive, concerned about being pulled out of the boat or that they would not be capable of winding in a tuna. After assuring the girls neither was going to occur or be a problem, tension eased on their faces and they sat back to relax in the comfort of the salon as the boat rode easily upon the gentle swells. It was going to be a long ride; the bite had been in The Norfolk the previous couple days, which was a seventy-five-nautical-mile run.

Although the Fisherman had gotten rods and lures ready the evening before, ballyhoo still needed to be rigged. During the next hour of running under lights at the cockpit rigging station, the men watched as the Fisherman's skilled hands rigged ballyhoo on 130-pound mono leaders with 8/0 J-hook rigs. Sea Witches and Ilanders were used to skirt the ballyhoo and turn them into colorful baits that hopefully no tuna could resist. Color often made a difference when it came to turning on a bite; pink, blue/white, and black/purple were favorites and always in a tuna spread first thing in the morning, along with a couple multi-colored spreader bars. Of course, on lucky days, tuna would eat anything that moved behind the transom—those were the days the Fisherman liked to see. On days when fish were lock-jawed or as light conditions changed, the color of skirts would be changed, often in hopes of enticing a bite. Rule of thumb is: darker-colored bait in morning or overcast days, with bright colors used in sunlight.

The boat just crossed the fifty-fathom line at the tip of Norfolk Canyon as morning broke.

From up on the bridge, the Captain yelled something as throttles were pulled back, causing the loud hum of twin Cumming diesels to quiet down as the boat slowed to trolling speed. It was the Fisherman's cue to get lines in the water; he had gone back in the cabin and was explaining to the charter how to fight tuna. The Fisherman preferred having females on a rod—they listened and did everything necessary to land a fish. Men, on the other hand, often had fishing experience and, while they might be good anglers, many had never fought anything larger than a salmon or striped bass and tried to horse-in or manhandle the tuna, which often ended in lost fish.

Winding in a tuna is basically easy: lift the rod tip to the 1:00 position, then lower the tip to 2:30 as line is recovered by the reel. Anglers just need to remember to begin winding before lowering rod tip, so not to create slack in the line—the number-one reason why fish are lost. And when the fish is taking drag, just wait and hold rod at the 2:00 position until the fish stops; then resume lifting and cranking. Let the reel's drag and rod pressure tire out the tuna.

Women were good at this; maybe it had something to do with following directions, or maybe they were just better listeners! The Fisherman walked out of the salon sliding door to set lines when the captain yelled down, "Saw tuna breaking water up ahead, hurry up, get lines in the water."

The diesels powering down drew the school's attention and they swung in unison towards the sound as the few remaining flying fish scattered. The commotion of bright-colored fish and squid jumping in and out of surface white water looked appetizing. Several tuna from the school flashed towards the surface with the rest in tow. This triggered the larger tuna to attack. Being larger and quicker, it was first to devour a brightly colored squid.

A beautiful morning brings hope for a successful day offshore.

"Fish on! Did you see the size of that explosion?" The Fisherman was not talking to anyone in particular, but his shout certainly got everyone's attention. As he was reaching for the rod bent over, the girl standing next to the fishing chair was instructed to sit.

Before the rod was out of its holder, the captain yelled down from above, "They're in the baits!"

At the same time, two more drags started screaming and the captain turned the boat to port, where the first fish hooked up was heading east, making line disappear very quickly off the fifty-wide Penn International.

"I'll keep boat in gear until you get everyone hooked up." Hooked up meant standup gear for the other two anglers. There were two fighting belts and harnesses hanging by the bait-rigging station, exactly for times like this. The first rod was placed in the chair's rod holder and the girl sitting was told to hang on to the rod for a moment. The Fisherman then asked who was standing up to fight the fish as he reached for the belts. The men looked at each other as the girls shook heads no. This was not a time for debate, the Fisherman tossed wraparound Action Belts to the two men standing closest and handed them fishing rods with one quick instruction, "Make sure lines do not cross!" Harnesses would be used later, if necessary.

The boat slowed; at this point no more fish needed to be hooked up. The cockpit was in almost total chaos as the two anglers crisscrossed back and forth at the transom, while shouting and raising lines to see who was over who and trying not to tangle in the girl's line, sitting in the fighting chair. The tuna had caught everyone by surprise and the cockpit was not ready for fishing. He asked the remaining crew with free hands to wind in remaining lines as he cleared the pit, took bungee cords off gaffs, and tied up loose ends.

Once hooks flying around on rods were secured, everyone was told to stand back out of the way. Landing one tuna at a time is difficult enough; landing three takes some luck—and extra bodies in the way didn't provide it. At one point, it appeared the two standup fish were about to be lost when lines became entangled. There are literally only seconds before heat builds up from friction when tangled lines are under tension, ending in line separation and language that should not be repeated around children. The Fisherman told the anglers to touch rod tips, this brings the twist in the lines right to the rod tips, where the lines twisted can be seen. The Fisherman then grabbed one rod from an angler, took it over top the other rod two times, and both lines were free. Rod was handed back to the angler and, being able to tell these two fish were not that large, the Fisherman left the men on their own and stood behind the girl, whispering in an ear exactly what she should do.

The Fisherman learned years before that yelling seldom worked when trying to give someone instructions; however, whispering in an ear always got the person's attention. The girl did exactly as told and, within a very short period of time, had a rhythm going of raising the rod and retrieving line. The other two anglers were doing good jobs as well, since the fish began cooperating and stayed on opposite sides of the boat. Ten minutes later, two yellowfin of about thirty-five pounds were gaffed and placed in the killbox on ice.

Meanwhile, morning sun glistened rainbows off sweat, which had broken out on the girl's forehead. She had an athletic build and the Fisherman accessed her ability as capable of landing the tuna. Often, on larger fish, the rod needed to be transferred from angler to angler as they tired. But she was relaxed with rod in hand and not fighting herself—only the fish. The husband asked after thirty

This angler did everything necessary to put a well-deserved yellowfin on the deck.

minutes if she wanted him to take over. Actually, the question was more like a statement and sounded condescending. The Fisherman answered for her, "She is doing great," and she was. Her smile indicated that it was appreciated the Fisherman handled the question. No doubt she would have given the rod up to the husband's request.

The yellowfin made several good runoffs, initially stealing fifty or more yards of line on each run that had been painfully recovered. The girl was told to use these brief periods to rest momentary and conserve energy before having to start raising the rod and cranking again. Little by little, she gained line inch-by-inch, and the runs became shorter indicating the fish was tiring. At one point, she asked for a sip of water, but other than that, stayed focused and determined to win the battle. She was fighting for bragging rights and for dinner; the tuna was fighting for its life. The crew offered words of encouragement as minutes passed. Finally, after an hour, the Fisherman got hands on the leader and sunk the gaff into a beautiful yellowfin.

While the crew was celebrating with high-fives, hugs, kisses, and slaps on the back, below the surface, with no food in sight, the school of tuna continued swimming northward looking for their next meal. Their numbers had been reduced by two and the straggler that had been shadowing them since South Carolina was no longer there.

Tackled !

⚓ **TROLLING RIGS**
⚓ **PUMPING/WORKING A ROD**
⚓ **MULTIPLE HOOKUPS**
⚓ **SAVING FISH ON CROSSED LINE**

Chapter 6

Beast of the Beach

Beach shark fishing technique

"Hey, what you doing next weekend? Thought we could all get together and go down Assateague and surf fish. Bought a new Kayak; want to try it out." It was one of the Fisherman's sons calling.

Several times each year, the family, along with friends, coordinated schedules to spend evenings at Assateague Island Nations Seashore Park—one of a handful of locations left on the East Coast where anglers can still drive on the beach after obtaining a yearly permit at the cost of $90. Bon fires are also permitted; food cooked on the beach over an open flame always tastes better for some reason. The Fisherman knew it would be a relaxing and fun evening watching the grandkids do all the things they do on a beach to keep busy, but the main reason for going was to fish—shark fish to be more precise. Several light surf outfits would be rigged with double hook bottom rigs for kingfish, croaker, or whatever other species roaming the surf that would fit in a frying pan. In addition, three heavier outfits would be dedicated toward sharks. A kayak would be used to paddle shark lines out past the breakers of the second sandbar, normally a couple hundred yards or so off the beach.

Over the years, sharks had been hooked that broke rods, straightened hooks, broke steel leaders, and spooled reels, leaving only imagination to determine how big they were. Of course, imaginations always said the sharks were massive. The Fisherman actually thought losing fish made for better storytelling than landing fish, which actually proved their size! While smaller dogfish sharks could be caught just about anytime, it was sand tigers they would be after. These normally made a showing on the far side of the outer sandbar around sunset. Once darkness fell, the sharks felt comfortable crossing the shallow water on top the sandbar and dined just off the beach in the troughs—sometimes caught within fifty feet of the beach. The best shark fishing was on an incoming tide right after sunset.

"Sure, tell everyone to meet here at the farm around four o'clock Saturday."

Saturday evening arrived and a group of twenty-five people squeezed into several four-wheel-drive trucks and headed to Assateague, driving onto the beach after deflating tires to eighteen pounds. Low tire pressure widens out tires, giving traction, and prevents sinking down in the soft sand.

While a beach may just look like breaking waves to the casual observer, the Fisherman learned over years to read the waves, which told him the characteristics of the bottom. He had a keen eye for locating holes and troughs that held schools of pan fish. But more importantly, he could locate cuts in the outer bar. These cuts were not always present, but after a storm or east wind that developed large waves and rough surf conditions coinciding with high tide, cuts normally could be found. Cuts form due to too much water building up between the shoreline and sandbar. To release pressure, a cut forms in the bar where water rushes back out to sea and washes sand out in the process, creating a channel or cut.

The Fisherman studied the breaking waves on the outer bar, looking for a section of wave that did not show white water cresting on top. If every wave rose up in one area without white water, when the rest of the waves showed white water coming up onto the bar, this meant that the part of the wave without white water was going over deeper water where a cut existed. Within the first couple miles driving down the beach, a cut was observed and fishing camp was set up for the evening.

While the kids started digging sand crabs, making sand castles, and swimming before the sun went down, light rod rigs were baited and cast out with strips of squid and cut mullet. These rods were staggered different distances from shore. Sometimes kingfish, also known as sea mullet or whiting, along with spot and croaker, would be mere feet off the beach, right behind the first breaker. Other times they were found further out, so rods fished bait in likely locations. Fish use the cut as a channel for swimming back and forth through the outer sandbar. There are times when it is hard to keep bait on hooks due to fish being so thick, like traffic at rush hour. This evening there was a good bite and everyone was having fun catching fish, even small ones!

As the sun moved westward, it was decided to set the shark lines. There is safety in numbers and two kayaks are used when possible. Just in case the person transporting the shark lines should become entangled, help is readily available. In addition, life jackets are always worn as a safety precaution.

With shark lines set, the men's attention shifted from the light lines to listening for a reel clicker to indicate a shark had picked up one of the baits.

Shark rigs are simple to construct: a fish finder is used for weigh/sinker attachment. This allows a bite without the shark feeling the weight. Normally sixteen ounces holds bottom, if rough, up to a couple pounds might be necessary. A 9/0 steel J-hook is attached to a five-foot piece of wire leader of number 12 Malin copper-colored wire with swivel at the other end. Hook and swivel are attached to wire with haywire twist. Solid wire leader prevents shark teeth from cutting through leader, unlike seven stranded wire where the shark tears one thin strand at a time until biting through. Swivel is crimped to the end of 130-pound wind-on leader. The 130-pound leader handles sharks that wrap themselves up in line. For bait, any of the smaller fish caught, like Spot, are used. The fish are sliced lengthwise to allow scent into the water before attaching to hook. If fish are not caught for bait, whole squid are backup bait on the hook.

The Fisherman used old trolling outfits for the sharks with 4/0 Penn Senator reels and occasionally Penn International 50 class outfits. All were spooled with fifty-pound monofilament line. Drag was preset at twenty pounds of straight pull on a scale. When fishing, the reel was not engaged on the Senator reels, only the clicker. When it was rough and waves pulled line off the Senators, a rubber band would be wrapped around the fishing line and pole adding additional tension. This still allowed the reel to be in free-spool and a shark could pick up bait, run, and swallow bait before reel was engaged and hook set. It was a system that had worked for years; more than once the Fisherman had chased a rod being dragged through the sand, down towards the surf's edge because a reel was left engaged. On the International reels, the drag lever adjusted tension as necessary.

It does not take large fish to put a smile on some anglers.

Caution needs to be used when setting shark lines, especially when trying to paddle past the breakers. Watch those hooks!

The bite was steady for spot and kingfish this evening. The wives and kids kept the men busy taking fish off and baiting hooks.

Time slipped by and conversation turned to past sharks that had been caught. The Fisherman recalled one story as a teenager many years past, when he and a buddy caught five sharks one evening, seven or eight feet long (no doubt more like four or five feet!). Not knowing any better about conservation, the sharks were left laying on the beach. A group of girls had stopped to talk after the sharks caught their attention. After that night, a shark was always on the beach and girls always seemed to stop and talk. There was hope that one of the chance meetings would turn into "more than an acquaintance," but the girls were always on vacation and lived hundreds of miles away in the big cities and a relationship never seemed to work out.

The story was interrupted by *click, click, click*! All eyes turned to see which rod was making sound, but the Fisherman's oldest grandson was quick and had rod in hand setting the hook.

It was a tug of war with the shark winning most of the time. During the fight, the sun drifted lower in the western sky behind the sand dunes to say good night.

The battle continued until floodlights were a necessity and turned on to illuminate the fishing area. Then, for what seemed no reason, the hook pulled! All the shark rods now needed to be reset, since they were wound in to check bait. It is very frustrating after rods sit for a period of time without any bites to wind in line and find no bait! It is a pain to set lines, but every hour, bait needs to be checked, even with no bites. The Fisherman glanced over at the guys examining the hook wondering why it pulled.

"Hey, who is paddling the lines out?"

Now total darkness engulfed the little beach camp. The fishing lights and fire provided a feeling of security, but outside this realm laid total blackness with the moonless night. Fishing on the dark side of the moon, the dark, black, eerie ocean showed no horizon and the ocean flashed teeth when white water from breaking waves glistened in the camp's light. No doubt images conjured up *Jaws*, with a shark large enough to swallow a kayak and person sitting on top in one easy gulp! Everyone glanced back and forth, but not a word was spoken.

In his younger days, the Fisherman took the lines out, but now felt it was the next generation's responsibility to handle the task. Finally, a nephew removed his cloak of fear and stepped forward, "I'll do it!"

Relief could be detected on faces and, while no one got down on one knee to show a sign of respect, the nephew certainly gathered everyone's admiration. Light sticks were attached to the life jacket and the kayak. And, with shark lines secured to the Kayak, it disappeared into the darkness.

When bait is being set, rods should be held in hand as line is fed out. The clicker is left on to prevent backlash. This is done during daylight or darkness. However, after dark, a whistle is added to the process. Once the line on the reel spool dwindles down, indicating how far bait is off the beach, the whistle is blown and a flashlight flicked on and off so the person in the kayak knows to drop lines over. It's a simple system, but it works. The light sticks could be observed closing in on the beach and, a couple minutes later, everyone resumed fishing conversations with cold drinks in hand. It was then, without warning, one of the drags started screaming. The Fisherman's oldest son set the hook, but the shark paid no attention and kept swimming with dinner in its mouth. Fortunately, the shark swam down the beach and not out to sea.

The Fisherman's grandson begins the task of fighting a decent-sized shark.

When the sun sets behind dunes, the best shark fishing begins.

It took a minute until the shark realized something was preventing it from swimming without restraint; so it did what fish do when fear is felt: it swam faster. Meaning the angler was in tow running down the beach, so not to be spooled. If wondering, yes, sand tigers can swim faster than a man can run! One of the trucks was started, turned on headlights, and began following the group of men running down the beach who pointed flashlights out over the ocean from time to time, looking for a tell-tale sign of the shark. Deciding its current direction was not working, the shark made a 180-degree turn and swam back up the beach. With no time to catch breath, the angler and everyone running behind turned around to retrace steps. The scene had the makings of a great Charlie Chaplin fishing movie. About the time the party arrived back near camp, the shark thought better of its escape plan and decided to swim back out over the outer sandbar. It was then the real combat began. Line gained and line lost was the story for the next half hour. Finally, the angler got the upper hand, and first glimpse of a fin and tail out of the water behind the breakers, under spotlights, provided approximate size. Shouting erupted, or it should be said *more* shouting erupted.

Landing a shark on the beach is different than on a boat. When the shark is close to shore, it gets caught up in breaking waves and pushed in towards the beach, at which time slack line must be taken up quickly. However, when the water from the breaking wave rushes back off the beach, it drags the shark (that is trying to swim back to the deeper water) and gives it that much more of an advantage. It is at this point that caution must be taken that pressure does not exceed the line's breaking strength, since the angler tries to hold the shark from getting back into deep water. Sharks can only be brought so far into the white water before someone has to "get" the shark. The Fisherman had been doing this since childhood and it was his job. Mostly it was his job because no one else wanted to get in the water with the shark.

Snapping teeth certainly get attention, but the tail needs to be taken into consideration as well. One slap across the leg has produced four-letter words on more than one occasion. A blunt gaff is used to beach the shark for photos before it is released to disappear into the darkness of the ocean.

The damp cool night air had arrived during all the commotion, producing a fog that settled in over the ocean. With no takers to paddle lines back out and the fire looking very inviting, another shark expedition was called a victory. The men joined the girls around the fire to roast more hot dogs, as tired kids fell asleep on blankets under the stars. A celebratory toast was given as drinks were raised to the "Beast of the Beach!"

Tackled!

⚓ **PRIME TIME TO FISH**
⚓ **SETTING LINES WITH KAYAK**
⚓ **LANDING SHARKS IN SURF**

The Fisherman's nephew heads off into blackness to set shark lines. Light sticks are attached to the kayak and there is a life jacket for safety.

The Fisherman's son cranks on a sand tiger as the Fisherman clears the other rod. Fishing at night requires good lighting (flashlights) once a shark is hooked.

Watch the toes!!!

Another trophy is about to be released. A blunt gaff head allows the shark to be pulled back into the breakers without injury.

Chapter 7
Should Have Been Here Yesterday!

Charter boat chunkin techniques for tuna

"I booked you for tomorrow." The Fisherman had his head down in an oversized, custom-built fish box scrubbing out slime and never saw nor heard the man walking down the dock.

After nine straight days of running offshore charters, the next day was eagerly being looked forward to as a day off, trying to catch up on chores around the farm. Unlike many jobs, there are no off days in the charter industry unless someone doesn't charter the boat or NOAA forecasts small-craft advisories. These advisories differ across the United States by region, but in the mid-Atlantic, small craft means wind or gust forecasted to be 22 knots (25 MPH) and/or waves from five to seven feet. In either case, sloppy seas are expected, if not downright dangerous conditions. Experience had taught that feet are better left on dry ground in these conditions. But summer had drifted into the dog days of August and the current stretch of nice weather was forecasted for the next couple days.

The Fisherman looked up to see a man's broad smile and, in hand, a booking receipt from the office; soapy hands were wiped off on blood-stained shirt before a firm handshake was offered and introductions made. The man went on to say that the last couple evenings he had come to the marina and watched boats weigh their catches. Every boat seemed to have tuna, but the Fisherman's boat out-fished all the others; he was impressed. It was true; the boat was on a hot streak and had high hook for three days running and the killbox was filled to capacity with fourteen this day. Yellowfin tuna were thick on a thirty-fathom lump locally nicknamed the Hot Dog for over a week. The Fisherman's chunkin skills, developed over many years, certainly were showing. Friendly competition existed among the charter fleet and, the past few evenings, at the Tiki Bar, the ice-cold beer had been on other captains' tabs gathering to discuss the day's catch.

The man continued in an excited tone, "I can't believe my luck; never thought you would be available when I walked in the charter office to book a boat!" The man booked as a single angler, which seldom occurred with the cost of charters skyrocketing due to surges in fuel price.

The Fisherman knew optimism was necessary when running offshore, but there was a fine line between optimism and counting on catching fish before they were iced down in a killbox. The next day was already producing an arm-weary, backbreaking day of catching tuna for the man. He was giving many pounds of fresh tuna steaks to neighbors, based on what was observed hanging on the scale the past couple days. The Fisherman had seen it time and again: several days of great fishing suddenly vanish. Overnight, baitfish may have migrated to another area, followed by the schools of tuna. Then again, it could be as simple as Lady Luck missed the boat when it pulled out of the slip. Whatever the reason for not being successful on those rare days, after years of charter fishing, the Fisherman knew that no one should ever count on catching fish when running offshore. This was delicately explained to put chances of success into proper perspective.

However, the man would have none of it. He laughed shaking his head from side to side, "I know we'll catch fish!"

The Fisherman didn't want to sound pessimistic and let the issue rest on the last statement, finishing the conversation with, "Be here at 3:30 a.m. Want to get out of the slip early; we'll give it our best shot."

The next morning, after running almost fifty miles in total darkness, the sun began to paint soft, pastel hues upon the eastern horizon as throttles were pulled back. A dozen boats were already jockeying for anchor positions on the two-mile-long by half-mile-wide lump.

The Fisherman knew that, over the next hour or so, a couple hundred boats would arrive. At one location on the lump, a knoll rose up to a depth of 118 feet; it was the Fisherman's favorite spot. Most boats tried to anchor at the exact location where they had heard, knew, or actually caught fish previously. The Fisherman thought it funny that anglers anchored in the same place in the middle of the ocean knowing tuna schools were always on the move. Nonetheless, it was the reason for risking damage to expensive props and struts running in the dark, long before the sun thought about waking up, to anchor at your primary location—not to mention a decent bite often occurs right at daybreak; the early bird often does get the worm! The GPS finally sounded the alarm, indicating that the boat had passed over the exact location near the top of the lump where fish were caught three days running. After allowing for drift and wind, the anchor was sent towards bottom.

Chunkin for tuna, while not a science, does lend itself, as does most fishing, to a right or wrong way to fish. This is why the statement is often heard, "Ten percent of fishermen catch ninety percent of the fish." Four fifty-class rods with wide spool Penn International reels would be used. Each rod would have bait set at different depths. The deep rod had been the most productive recently and used two eight-ounce egg sinkers on the main line with a six-foot, fifty-pound fluorocarbon leader with 13/0 circle hook. The leader was attached to the main line by a 100-pound spro barrel swivel. Since tuna are often leader shy, egg sinkers are placed twenty-five feet above the barrel swivel and prevented from sliding down the fishing line by using a #64 rubber band tied tightly to line. Whole butterfish are typically used as bait on the deep line, with a circle hook embedded out of sight. The bait is rigged by taking the circle hook in the mouth, out a gill, under the fish and back in the opposite gill. The hook is then hidden in the stomach with only the point of the hook exposed.

Once satisfied the hook was embedded properly, the Fisherman sent the first rig towards bottom. There is a trick to setting deep lines: they must be let down extremely slow, so the bait does not wrap and tangle around the main fishing line. Once the sinker hits bottom, five cranks were taken in on the reel, placing the bait about twelve feet off the bottom and hopefully away from bait-eating bottom-dwelling creatures. The deep rod is fished directly under the boat. Satisfied with the bait placement, the rod was placed in a holder and drag setting adjusted. The drag on deep lines is set at fighting pressure, which is thirty percent of breaking-line strength. With so much line out, there's plenty of slack for tuna to swim and swallow the bait. Circle hooks are preferred over J-hooks, since the fish are able to hook themselves. The Fisherman proceeded to rig two more rods in the same

Another beautiful sunrise as anchor is about to find bottom. Pulling out of the slip at "O'Dark-thirty" allows anglers to set up at prime locations.

manner, but used lighter weights and added floats to suspend bait. The next bait was set at a depth of thirty feet and located sixty feet behind the boat with a two-ounce egg sinker. The third rod set at sixty feet depth and placed 100 feet behind the boat with eight ounces. The fourth rod is known as a floater line. A weight is not necessary with little or no current. Otherwise, a one-half to one-ounce egg sinker is added to keep the bait a few feet under the surface. However, on this particular day, with very little current, no weight was required. This rod had thirty-pound fluorocarbon leader, since the bait was presented high in the water column, allowing penetrating light to make the leader visible. The bait on the floater would be a chunk of butterfish and drifted forty feet behind the boat with an extremely light drag setting on the reel. Drag was so light that when a tuna picked up the piece of bait, it would not feel resistance, often the cause for dropped bait and missed opportunity. The hook would be hidden to the best of the Fisherman's ability in the chunk of bait.

Chunkin gets its name from cut-up pieces of butterfish (chunks) that are constantly thrown in the water, producing a chum line slowly sinking behind the boat. Butterfish come in twenty-five pound boxes known as flats; the Fisherman normally used three flats during a full day of fishing. While a knife worked well to cut each butterfish into five or six pieces, it didn't have a conscience or care when it cuts fingers. The Fisherman learned this the hard way years before on a choppy day. Now a pair of scissors was used to cut chunks on the rocking boat. Pieces of chunk are spaced about every five feet apart when thrown over to coax tuna into coming behind the transom to feed. Even after a tuna is hooked up, it is very important to keep the chunk line going to keep the school of tuna around the boat, creating additional bites and multiple hookups. However, with only one angler aboard, tuna would be hooked and caught one at a time this day.

An hour after setting lines, the man patiently sat watching for a rod to double over and the sweet song of a reel's drag to fill the air. From time to time, yelling and shouting could be heard off in the distance indicating a hookup. Scanning the horizon, excited anglers could be observed gathering near the transom of a boat as a tuna was gaffed, but it was a rare occurrence. The sonar's screen remained void of any type of activity under the Fisherman's boat.

During idle times like these, the Fisherman passed time learning about clients. Everyone had different backgrounds and he enjoyed hearing their life stories. This day the man explained how he had bought a small used-car lot in New York and built the business into three large dealerships. He and his wife recently bought an oceanfront condo and expected to spend a lot of weekends charter fishing. Repeat clientele is a large part of the charter business; a successful day can turn into many more paydays. Word of mouth quickly spreads the name of a charter boat after a successful day. But the Fisherman didn't want the man to catch tuna just for this reason; he was a pleasure to have onboard and wanted him to experience what it was like going into battle with a tuna screaming line off a reel. In addition, his work ethics and personal pride demanded the very best effort every day.

Hour after hour passed, conversations turned to sports, weather, politics, and finally back to fishing and why the tuna weren't biting. Every trick the Fisherman knew was tried, including hand feeding. This is where the floater line is dropped behind the transom along with big handfuls of chunk. The line is then free-spooled out a couple hundred yards, so the baited hook drifts out, mixed in with massive amounts of chunk. Often, tuna stay 100 feet or more behind the boat gobbling up chunks. When this occurs, hand feeding often is the ticket to success—but not on this day.

Another trick is to take a middle depth line and locate the bait right above or below the thermocline. The thermocline is the stratification of seawater, where colder temperatures from the deep separate from the warmer water above. By turning up the gain on the sonar, clutter appears showing the thermocline depth. Often, tuna feed near one or the other side of the thermocline, but mostly on the cold side where water is clearer. Bait was positioned on both sides several times with negative results. Current below the surface often spins bait. Tuna do not like spinning bait! To counter this, lines were free-spooled out 100 yards before winding back to the boat and repeating. This way, the bait did not spin as it drifted along with the current. Unfortunately, that didn't work either. A couple Shimano jigging rods were dug out of the cabin and both the Fisherman and man worked jigs covering the whole water column until arms felt as if they were going to fall off...to no avail.

As the sun made its way into the western part of the sky, optimism waned. One by one, charter boats pulled anchor and headed towards port. Radio communication was very light, a sure indication that it was a slow day of fishing. There would be very few tuna flags flapping in the wind as boats came through the inlet this day. Onshore observers line the inlet each evening to watch boats return and would no doubt comment how it was a bad day offshore.

Finally, the Fisherman called it a day and squared everything away before pulling anchor. The tired man was invited up on the flying bridge, something that seldom occurred, for the long ride back to the docks. This two-hour period was reserved each day as private thinking time for the Fisherman. He sat back, relaxed, and enjoyed observing nature's wonders while deep in thought. Shearwaters were able to soar inches off the water surface without ever dipping a wing. Tiny, fragile-looking storm petrels fluttered about on the ocean's surface, appearing to walk on water. The Fisherman found it fascinating how petrels could survive hurricane-force winds without coming onshore. Water spouting from whales and pods of porpoises jumping were common sights as the boat tried to catch up with each day's setting sun. The drone of twin diesels normally drowned out client's conversations below until the fish box cover was lifted, producing congratulatory shouts and the slapping of backs. This normally produced another round of beer extracted from a cooler. However, there was none of that this day and there would be no *oohs* and *aahs* from people gathered around the Tiki Bar to watch tuna hoisted from the killbox to be weighed, butchered into steaks, and packaged.

Once ropes secured the boat in its slip, the engine's rpm gauges fell to zero. There was a moment of silence before the man reached out his hand. "I know you tried your best." The Fisherman felt bad on a rare day when no fish were caught, but forced a smile and stated, "You should have been here yesterday!"

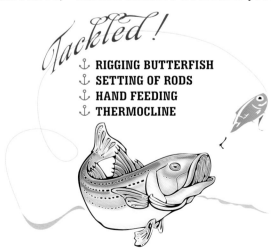

Tackled!

⚓ RIGGING BUTTERFISH
⚓ SETTING OF RODS
⚓ HAND FEEDING
⚓ THERMOCLINE

Chapter 8
White Marlin

How to rig ballyhoo on circle hooks and using dredges

The phone call came after dinner, just as the Fisherman propped his feet up to get comfortable in his old rocker to watch the evening news. "Hey can you fish tomorrow? Owner wants to give those whites a shot; need a second mate to help out."

The captain calling ran a beautiful, fifty-eight-foot, private Sportsfisherman for a well-to-do owner.

"Sure; what time you pulling out? Okay, see you at the boat 3:45." With that, the Fisherman turned off the TV and began packing a lunch and throwing odds and ends into a duffle bag. No doubt the owner would have breakfast and lunch provided, but the Fisherman always liked having his own brown bag along.

It was early fall, the best time of the year to fish for white marlin. In late summer, along the mid-Atlantic, the bite heated up, but not until those first few chilly nights of fall did it really turn red hot in most years. Always seemed strange to the Fisherman all the money spent trying to catch fish that were released. But marlin fishermen were like that. It was the challenge of the battle and being hypnotized by their aerobatics, which, at times, seemed to defy gravity. Once bitten by the marlin bug, it would probably be a lot cheaper for an angler to become a heroin addict. They were going to need a marlin fix often and it was not going to be cheap. Dedicated marlin fishermen did not want to catch tuna, dolphin, or wahoo. They were content to troll all day for one or two shots at catching a white or blue marlin.

But that was not going to be the case the next day—at least it shouldn't have been. The bite had been "epic" the previous couple days and there was no reason to think otherwise for the next one. At least, that is how the Fisherman felt—if you were not going to be optimistic about fishing, not a lot of sense in going!

The alarm clock sounded early and, soon after, the Fisherman was in the cockpit with the other mate rigging baits as the boat pulled out of the slip. At least four dozen naked ballyhoo were needed to be rigged for circle hooks to begin the day. There is no doubt circle hooks increase hook-up percentage over J-hooks when billfishing. And since the NMFS rule making circle hooks mandatory for billfish tournaments, it only made sense to practice with them during recreational fishing.

The Fisherman tried several ways to rig ballyhoo on circle hooks over the years and finally settled with the method most professional captains and mates used. Leaders were constructed using Eagle Claw 8/0 circle hooks snelled to a six-foot piece of eighty-pound monofilament leader, which attached to a wind-on leader. Why snell the hook? Snelling does not allow the hook to twist or slip on the leader. This results in the hook being stationary when coming to the corner of the fish

This type of action is what creates an addiction to white marlin fishing.

mouth, which transcends into a better hook-up percentage. (For instruction video on how to snell a hook, go online to YouTube at the following link: www.youtube.com/watch?v=ExppbseEu0g or search "John Unkart" on YouTube to find the crimping instructional video, along with other videos by the author on rigging and offshore fishing techniques.)

The ballyhoo had already been thawed and were in saltwater with ice to toughen up the skin. Quickly, the Fisherman and mate removed eyes; if not, water collected in eye sockets when trolling and ballooned them, not allowing the bait to swim properly. Next, the waste from the intestines and stomach was removed by laying the ballyhoo flat after a small incision was made at the anus, easing the task of removing of innards. A thumb on the body cavity/stomach area pushed towards the tail, using slight pressure, removed the waste.

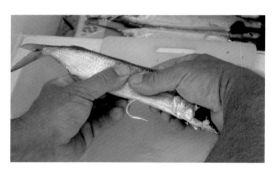

Next, the back/spine was made flexible by "popping" the scales along the spine. Using a thumb and forefinger, the spine was pinched slightly from the head towards the tail. The Fisherman knew that one must be careful not to apply too much pressure or the skin would tear. But after years of "popping" the spine on thousands of ballyhoo, it came as second nature. Popping the spine was the difference between having a ballyhoo appear to be "swimming" or "pulled" through the water.

The ballyhoo was next made flexible by gently bending in half—once again, being careful not to tear/rip the skin.

It took about a half-hour to prep all the ballyhoo; then rigging began. A two-foot piece of wax rigging line was folded in half and inserted through half-ounce egg sinkers. Normally, half-ounce were used on "dink" baits, which are small ballyhoo. On medium size ballyhoo, three-quarter-ounce was used. A half hitch was tied in the wax line beforehand to assist in the next step.

The loop of wax line was slid over the head of the ballyhoo and placed behind the gill plates. Egg sinker was centered under the gills. The half hitch tied earlier came up over top of the bill. The two tag ends were pulled to tighten the half hitch down over the nose and secure egg sinker in place. A second half hitch was then tied to prevent slipping off the top of the nose. The tag ends were then run through the eyes, creating an "X" on top of the head.

The tag ends came out of the eye sockets and were tied below the gill plates to keep them closed and to secure the egg sinker.

As each ballyhoo was prepared, it was put in a tray on ice in the bait box. Later, when the ballyhoo was attached to the fishing line, all that was required was running the circle hook under the center knot of the "X" on the head of the ballyhoo. It was a simple rigging process that worked. (See Chapter 34 for a trick on how to skirt a circle hook rig ballyhoo.)

When bait preparation was finished, the two dredges were put together with ballyhoo salted down the evening before.

Using a rag dampened with salt water beneath and on top of Ballyhoo for dredge prevents them from drying out overnight if rigged the night before.

Building a Dredge

When pulling a natural ballyhoo dredge, it is necessary to prepare the ballyhoo the night before and to salt down to toughen up for a day of trolling. A dredge of natural ballyhoo can be quickly snapped together, once ballyhoo are rigged on dredge wires. The skirts are an option, but the Fisherman believes the flash adds fish-drawing ability. The wires can be purchased at any tackle shop and ballyhoo dredge wires, made as shown, using one-ounce egg sinkers.

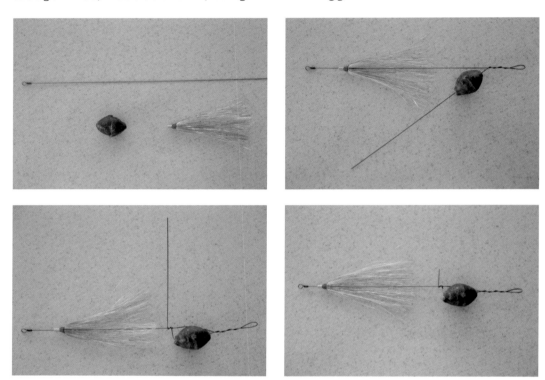

To rig ballyhoo, the end of wire is inserted under gill with the pin coming up through the head and protruding from the top.

A rubber band is wrapped about the head of ballyhoo to secure on pin.

Once rigged, place ballyhoo in bait box and salt down, covering with damp saltwater rag.

When getting ready to fish, each ballyhoo needs only to be snapped onto the dredge.

With all tasks completed, the two mates sat back and relaxed for the rest of the run, discussing different methods used to catch a variety of fish. One thing the Fisherman always said, "Every day fishing is a learning experience." And he took every opportunity to pick the brain of other captains and mates—or anyone else who would share fishing information.

Finally, the boat slowed and the captain said to set the spread. This consisted of four lines: two flat lines and two lines run from outriggers. In addition, two rods were set up as pitch baits for when marlin were drawn to either of the two dredges or teasers that were being used. In that case, the bait-and-switch would be implemented.

The boat was in seventy fathoms on the edge of Poorman Canyon, and shearwaters were diving and feeding heavily on baitfish being balled up by packs of white marlin. Every time the Fisherman looked to the horizon, a white marlin could be seen tailing. It took all of about two minutes before the first marlin of the day was hooked and, shortly thereafter, released by the owner. Fortunately, the owner invited a buddy along, since there were many double and triple hookups. It would be historic in terms of white marlin caught this day in the mid-Atlantic and records of catch and release fell from Ocean City, Maryland, to Virginia Beach, Virginia. The Fisherman and other mate each set new personal records this day with seventeen white marlin released in non-stop action. The count of white marlin bites was lost at thirty-five, plus additional fish raised that were only window shopping.

On the ride back to port, the owner was ecstatic, his buddy was thrilled, the captain was euphoric; down in the cabin, the Fisherman and boat's mate were fast asleep…dog-ass tired!

This happy crew racked up seventeen white marlin releases this day, contributing to a day in history known as the greatest white marlin bite ever recorded from Ocean City, Maryland, to Virginia Beach, Virginia.

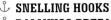

Tackled!

- SNELLING HOOKS
- BALLYHOO PREPARATION AND RIGGING
- CREATING DREDGE WIRES
- FOUR-LINE SPREAD

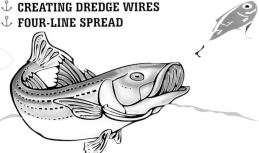

Chapter 9
Just Never Know

Offshore adventures that ended in catching fish unexpectedly

Sometimes, the best catches are ones that aren't supposed to occur.

"GOT ONE!"
There was a good bend in the rod and, from the look of it, another decent-sized golden tilefish would eventually break surface water and be put on ice with others in the killbox. A few yards of line was gained before the fish went back to the bottom in 760 feet of water, typical behavior of a large golden tile when hooked. The rod was pumped and, as line started being retrieved, a sideways angle to the line began to develop. The fish was clearly not directly under the boat, but swimming along the bottom—something that, out of the hundreds of golden tilefish the Fisherman had caught or witnessed caught, never occurred. Whatever was at the end of the line in the depths of the ocean clearly had everyone scratching their heads as to what it might be.

Thirty minutes later, with no line gained, the scratching went to bewildered looks and negative head nods. There were many guesses as to what had swallowed one of the whole squids on the circle hook bottom rig, with swordfish being the number one possibility—although everyone on board knew swordfish were not normally found in this shallow of water during hours of daylight. The fish strung out over 300 yards of line at one point and was near the surface before going back down to the bottom… again. Up and down, back and forth, the fish swam as the fight continued for another hour. The Shimano Torsa 20 class reel, Trevela rod, and Fisherman's youngest son, were being put to the test. Finally, the fish momentarily surfaced thirty yards from the boat.
"Is that a yellowfin?"
"Can't be."
"Sure looks like one."
"You sure?"
"No way."
A few minutes later, the fish surfaced again closer to the boat.
"Well I'll be; it *is* a yellowfin!"
After the tuna was gaffed, the reason it was so hard to land was evident. The tuna ate the bottom squid bait on a four-foot-long four-hook bottom rig. The top hook had foul hooked in the tuna's tail. Every time the angler lifted on the rod, it pulled the tuna's tail upwards, and with every tail thrust, the tuna forced itself downward towards bottom!
Exactly what was a yellowfin tuna doing feeding on the bottom in over 700 feet of water? More puzzling: What was this keen-eyed predator of the ocean doing inhaling

The Fisherman's son with yellowfin hooked on a golden tilefish rig in almost 800 feet of water!

a large hook clearly visible on 250-pound leader Material, which underwater looks like the diameter of rope to a fish? Of course, these questions cannot be answered, but certainly illustrate the point that anglers never know what they might catch and thus should be prepared for the unexpected.

Every offshore angler gets antsy each spring waiting to get offshore into the deep. Cooped up all winter reading magazines, books, and watching fishing shows only goes so far in satisfying the fishing appetite. Once the boat is uncovered, waxed, and prepared for the first trip, it is agony waiting until the weather and catch forecast looks good.

And so it was with the Fisherman and a few of his buddies. There were phone calls one day in early May: "Hey, want to go fishing?"

The Fisherman received the same reply from everyone—a resounding *yes*. Everyone knew the water was cold and very few (as in almost *no*) fish had been caught offshore yet, with the exception of a few sharks and bluefish. But that didn't make any difference with a forecast of flat, calm seas and a hint of summer in expected temperatures the upcoming Saturday. The GPS was dialed in on a temperature change of two degrees, according to sea surface temperature shot, seventy miles to the east of the inlet. While there was a boatload of optimism being voiced, deep down each angler knew chances were slim of catching any fish. But slim meant…there was a *chance*!

Arriving at the break, the Fisherman put out a mixed spread to cover any species that might have wandered this far north in the sixty-two-degree water. A 3½ drone spoon was down off a planer, often an early season bluefin who doesn't mind tolerating cooler water finds this appealing. Two spreader bars, along with an assortment of skirted ballyhoo, and a naked ballyhoo on a flat line, filled out the eight-line spread. While the crew was discussing how great it was to be back out on the water, the rod with a blue/white Ilander skirted over medium-sized ballyhoo went off. The first fish of the year was hooked up; the shouts of joy probably could be heard onshore. Shortly thereafter, the first yellowfin of the year was gaffed.

The Fisherman wondered how one small yellowfin could make a crew excited beyond imagination. But then again, he could feel the excitement as well; the season had officially begun. The lines were reset and trolling resumed; shortly thereafter, another yellowfin joined the first in the killbox. All was quiet until after noon when a marlin suddenly popped up behind the flat line.

Now the Fisherman was excited, it was his favorite fish that swam in the ocean to chase. He shouted, "Marlin left flat line!" But before anyone else moved from his seat, the helm was vacant and the Fisherman was free-spooling the naked ballyhoo. Five seconds later, the drag was slowly engaged and the circle hook found the corner of the mouth. Rod was handed off to a lifelong friend as the fish took to the sky.

"Look at the size of that marlin!"

The billfish had taken a 30 class outfit and gave the angler all he could handle. But patience and persistence paid off. Forty minutes later, the Fisherman had leader in hand, at which point it was an official catch. Being the first marlin of the year, it was brought onboard for photos. The cold ocean water of spring had somehow given up a decent day of fishing offshore.

Another year, the calendar showed spring was just around the corner, but Old Man Winter still had a surprise up his sleeves and dumped several inches of snow on the mid-Atlantic the night before. The Fisherman always enjoyed the solitaire of the beach after a snow.

"Think I am going to ride over to the beach, want to come along?" The Fisherman posed the question to his wife, knowing the answer before even being asked.

The first yellowfin of the season did not have to be large to make everyone smile.

What a great way to kick off the first offshore trip of the season.

The famous Ocean City, Maryland, boardwalk; you can almost smell Thrasher's French Fries.

This north jetty light tower was swept away in a nor'easter a couple weeks after this snow.

Sunrise over boat ramp at Wachapreague, Virginia.

The Fisherman's nephew assists his wife with landing a catch of bluefish, red rosie, and spiny dogfish. Multiple species caught on the same drop occurs often.

Several bluefish were caught this day feeding right on bottom with golden tilefish. Fisherman's buddy with a nice double header.

"No thanks; go ahead and freeze your butt off."

The Ocean City, Maryland, boardwalk, world renown for Thrasher French Fries and as a summer resort playground for tens of thousands of children and adults each day, was all but deserted this morning.

The Fisherman wandered over near the inlet and leaned against the sea wall railing, watching gulls gliding back and forth a few feet off the water over the mouth of the inlet in search of breakfast.

The birds probably want to see breaking fish almost as much as I do, he thought. It would be another few weeks before striped bass migrated this far north, with blues a couple weeks behind them. Looking at the tip of the south jetty, his imagination ran wild: a school of silversides exploded from the ocean where the current swirled on the outgoing tide, caused from rocks a few feet beneath the surface. The boat idling in gear held it in place, as casts were made to where the evading baitfish tried to fly in order to avoid death. On each cast there was no telling which predator species would inhale the bucktail and bend the spinning rod over double. The Fisherman was lost in reminiscing thoughts of fishing trips that produced rockfish, bluefish and sea trout, caught over the years at that jetty tip, before realizing an hour of life had slipped away. The trip to the beach only made the wait to go fishing more unbearable.

When the Fisherman walked in the door, his wife said, "Your nephew called; wants to know if you want to go fishing." This time it was the Fisherman's wife who knew the answer before the reply!

Cabin fever apparently was an epidemic, as everyone called jumped at the opportunity to fish with no reports of any fish caught offshore. Early Saturday morning, the nephew's boat launched at Wachapreague, Virginia, for a deep-drop trip to Norfolk Canyon.

A flatter ocean could not be imagined on the ride to the canyon. Every few miles, another layer of clothing needed to be shed. Finally, the throttles were pulled back over a location where golden tilefish and grouper were caught during summer. An assortment of bait headed towards the bottom 800 feet below. It took all of about five seconds once bait hit bottom for rods to bend. A variety of fish were caught, drop after drop, all unforeseen since expectations were not set high. Actually, there was little hope *any* fish were going to be caught, other than maybe spiny dogfish that appreciate colder water. This day was going to be little more than an opportunity to get out of the house and take the first long ride of the year on a nice day. However, every long crank brought up surprises. Bluefish were feeding on the bottom, along with the sharks and black-belly red rosies.

Golden tilefish occasionally managed to grab a hook from time to time and ended up in the killbox as well.

Two days earlier, the snowfall made fishing seem as far away as possible. However, offshore, the warm Gulf Stream made the air pleasant in the mid-60s. Now, every year when daffodils think about busting through snow to greet spring, a boatload of buddies get an early start on the offshore fishing season, never knowing what might be caught.

Tackled!

⚓ **EARLY SEASON COOL WATER TROLLING SPREAD**
⚓ **DEEP DROPPING EARLY IN SEASON**

Chapter 10

Spring Rock

How to troll for striped bass with planer boards

Walnut-sized brains somehow allowed the fish to know where they were bred and born. After wintering off the coasts of Virginia and North Carolina, as April's sun warmed the ocean, millions swam towards their main breeding grounds on the East Coast to the Chesapeake Bay. Here, in the 150 freshwater tributaries that feed the Chesapeake, the striped bass would spawn and deposit eggs so the circle of life continued. A mature female weighing thirty pounds is capable of dropping in excess of five million eggs. The importance of the Chesapeake breeding grounds cannot be over emphasized: it produces about ninety percent of the striped bass for the entire East Coast. After spawning, most of the mature fish leave the bay and continue north, spending summer along the northeast coast and Bay tributaries—until winter's approach, when Mother Nature releases harsh cold winds out of the north, sending water temperatures plummeting and schools of baitfish scurrying south. The striped bass follow their meals, finally arriving somewhere around Virginia in late December, where, once again, they take up residence and wait on the spring migration.

Biologists call the species *Morone saxatilis*, but up and down the East Coast the fish are referred to as striped bass, stripers, or rockfish by most anglers. However, for fishermen raised and born on the Chesapeake, the fish are simply called "rock." Commercial waterman, recreational fisherman, boat owners, and charter fleets scattered up and down the Chesapeake all count on the fish returning to the Bay each year. The rock not only provides recreational fishing enjoyment, but also the bread and butter for a commercial seafood industry putting food on the table for millions of consumers. A fishing industry worth millions in tax revenue for the state of Maryland is based on this fish.

There was a time when shad entered the Chesapeake Bay each spring as well, a favorite food source for the rock. But years of pollution from urban runoff and dams built on the Susquehanna River diminished their migrations to fresh-water breeding areas. After the shad's disappearance, it's no coincidence that schools of baitfish (menhaden) enter the Chesapeake Bay each spring. Mother Nature makes sure there is balance and abundant nourishment for the rock.

Once hatching, the juvenile rockfish take up residence in the Bay for the first couple years of life, while feasting and growing on the plentiful food supply. They then leave and do not return again until obtaining spawning size, which is normally five to eight years of age for the females and two to three years for the males. It is then the fish join the yearly migration and return each year to where they once drifted on the currents as eggs, hatching about eighty hours later. This spawning cycle occurs because a meteor picked a minuscule location on the surface of the earth to impact 35 million years ago, creating what is now known as the Chesapeake Bay, the largest estuary in the United States.

Another predator invades the Chesapeake each spring known as fishermen. Tens of thousands pull covers off boats, wash and wax hulls, de-winterize engines, and clean up fishing gear in preparation of the rocks' arrival, which normally begins in April when water temperature approaches fifty degrees.

The Fisherman grew up on the Chesapeake Bay, as did his father and grandfather. He had seen the rock devastated back in the late 1970s and early 1980s, to the point where fishing was shut down for four years, beginning in 1985. Although the Fisherman was often at odds with biologists, this was one time they agreed. The four-year moratorium took fishing pressure off the remaining stock and allowed the species to regenerate back to numbers the Fisherman was told stories about as a youngster. It was a true success story of replenishing rock in the Chesapeake and along the entire East Coast.

This spring, one of the Fisherman's grandsons turned seven and would begin to learn the techniques of trolling for rock as part of the family heritage that had been handed down. Over decades, the methods and lures changed from time to time for catching the fish during their spring spawning run. As a child, the Fisherman first learned how to troll large bucktails and red surgical hoses with a piece of wire inside, bent correctly to provide attractive swimming action. After that, it was #19 Tony Acetta spoons and L.B. Huntington's size 4½ Drone spoons with inline sinkers that took the Chesapeake by storm. The 1970s saw Crippled Alewive 11/0 spoons in silver or white. They were all the rage and trolled up and down the Chesapeake behind every transom. And while every one of these methods still caught fish, the recent trend was using planer boards, enabling a dozen or more rods to be trolled creating a large spread, even from small boats. Planer boards are typically constructed using three boards of various sizes. Angles cut on the front of the boards force them to pull away from the boat with forward momentum. This allows fishing lines to be attached and trolled off the line, connecting the planer boards to the boat.

While spoons and hoses could be used, they have an inherited craving to tangle. So anglers went back to the first lure the Fisherman learned how to troll: the bucktail. It pulled straight and reduced the number of four-letter words necessary when untangling a twisted ball of monofilament fishing line due to spinning lures crossing. The Fisherman rigged rods for the most part with tandem bucktails in conjunction with six- or nine-inch sassy shads. Several colors of bucktails and sassy shad had been tried over the years, with chartreuse, yellow, and white the clear favorites. The bucktails ranged in weight from two to ten ounces, with a lighter bucktail used on the top leader, which was thirteen feet in length. The heavier bucktail ran below to prevent tangles on a five-foot leader. The bucktails were attached to a three-way swivel, which was attached to the fishing line.

Another recent lure gaining popularity by anglers is the Umbrella rig. The lure works on the principle: survival of the fittest. When feeding, fish normally attack the last fish/bait struggling to keep up behind a school of baitfish. This is what the Umbrella rig represents. It consists of several rubber sassy shad on wire spreaders, imitating a school of menhaden. At the rear, a single bucktail with sassy shad is attached.

Finally, a day the Fisherman had been waiting for arrived. "Hey, wake up; want to go fishing today with Daddy and Pop?"

Flags on planer boards help other boaters observe them in choppy water and indicates to stay clear.

Typical springtime rock that found a tandem bucktail rig to its liking.

It was the Fisherman's son waking up his grandson. As a family tradition, the young man got to miss a day of school. With no previous discussion about fishing, he was awakened bright and early for the surprise fishing trip. As his grandson raced down the living-room staircase, his feet barely touched a step. The Fisherman recollected those special days when, as a child, *he* got to miss school and spend the day with Dad fishing on the Chesapeake for spring rock; a smile crossed his face.

The boat was ready to go at the end of the pier, already loaded up with rods, tackle, lunch, etc. Within twenty minutes of the boy climbing out of bed, dock lines were cast off and boat waves interrupted the calmness of early morning on the Chesapeake Bay. The Bay Bridge loomed to the south through a morning fog that had settled upon the water during the cool dampness of night. Trolling would begin in an area along the Eastern side of the Chesapeake known as the mile markers off Kent Island. Kent Island has the distinction of being the largest island in the Chesapeake Bay and once home to the Matapeake Indian tribe. In 1631, William Claiborne established the first European settlement on the Island, which eventually led to becoming the state of Maryland.

The Fisherman found the rich history of the Maryland Eastern Shore very interesting. Stories of Indians forging for soft crabs in grass beds would be shared with the boy, but there was no time this morning. Throttles were pulled back and, as the boat slowed, planer boards were deployed.

Lines attached to planer boards need to be pulled from a high location on a boat, such as a T-top or off the upper structure of the boat. This creates a downward slope, easing the deployment of fishing lines. But more importantly, the angle keeps the planer board's towline up and out of the water.

The boy watched intently as lines were set—not realizing he was actually learning. He was often on the pier and met the boat when his dad and pop returned from a day of fishing. The glistened rock in afternoon sun, when held up for photos, created an undeniable desire to grow up quick, so he could go along on the trips down the Bay. Hearing the phase "when you're old enough" did little to ease the pain of not being able to go along. He'd fished for white perch and spot. But, to catch a rock like those he saw and listened to in stories told when fishermen gathered and discussed trolling, was his dream.

Now that the day had arrived, excitement of being on the boat for his first spring rock trip was not contained. He bombarded his father and grandfather with question after question about why they did things the way they did.

Spring rock often feed near the surface, since schools of menhaden find the sun's surface-warming effect to their liking, meaning lures need to be near the surface on most days. The Fisherman set the fishing line closest to the starboard planer's towline at a distance of forty feet. The next line was set at sixty feet and the third at eighty feet. On the opposite side of the boat, the lures were set at fifty, seventy-five, and 100 feet. Depending on weight of bucktails, they ran anywhere under the surface from four to twelve feet. The remaining four lines were set deeper and trolled directly behind the boat from gunwale rod holders. Sixteen-ounce sinkers were used on two Umbrella rigs to place them at depths of fifteen and twenty-five feet, almost right below boat. Two more lines were set behind the boat at 125 and 150 feet. This ten-rod setup accounted for many fish over the years in the cooler. If fishing was slow, another four rods could be added, two on each planner line—but only if necessary.

With lines set, the boat zigzagged along an edge off Kent Island where the depth dropped from thirty to sixty feet of water. Sonar indicated there were rock

Standard double bucktail rig; heavier bucktail is attached to shorter leader, which is five feet; lighter bucktail on longer thirteen foot leader.

One of the most popular lures currently trolled on the Chesapeake Bay for spring rockfish, the Umbrella Rig.

There are two methods of attaching fishing lines to the planer line. The first is to use spring-type clips.

When line keeps "popping" out of clip, a rubber band rectifies the situation.

The second method is to utilize rubber bands and D-clips.

A rubber band wrapped several times around fishing line before being placed in D-clip holds line in correct position.

Both clips accomplished the same thing: holding a deployed lure at a predetermined distance, which is marked on the fishing line of each rod. When using spring clips, fishing line only needs to be inserted—tension holds it in place. Although, when heavy bucktails are used, a rubber band wrapped about the clip keeps the fishing line from snapping out when planer boards jump around as they hit the waves. When using the rubber-band method, the band is twisted around the fishing line several times and hooked in the D-ring. When a rock is hooked, the rubber band breaks.

Once a lure is set at proper distance from the boat and secured in clip, the clip is attached to the planer towline. As line comes off the fishing reel, the clip slides down the planer line. When satisfied with positioning, reel is engaged and rod placed in holder. The rod with bait set close to the planer board needs to be the highest rod on the boat in a holder. This allows the fishing line to clear the others after a bite, so the fish can be wound in without disturbing the other rods.

and baitfish all along the edge. No doubt it seemed like a lifetime to the boy, but finally the waiting was over and the sound of a line snapped. He got to feel the weight and pull of a big rock. Fifteen minutes later (with a little help from Dad), the boy's first spring rock eased into the net. The experience of catching the fish now etched into his memory, never to be forgotten and only to increase in size over years when told in stories. The boy was now a Chesapeake Bay Trophy Rock Fisherman.

Tackled!

⚓ **TANDEM BUCKTAIL RIGGING**
⚓ **UMBRELLA RIG**
⚓ **SETTING LINES**

The Fisherman's grandson with his first two trophy rock!

Chapter 11
Billfish Tournament Tactics

Technique strategy when participating in billfish tournaments

The White Marlin Open; Pirates Cove Billfish Tournament; Mid-Atlantic 500, Big Rock; and Virginia Beach Billfish Tournament are but a few of the popular tournaments available to Atlantic billfish anglers. With possibilities of big paydays looming offshore, the competition is tough, drawing world-class fishermen to many of the tournaments. Can offshore, recreational, weekend fishermen have a shot at going to the scales and collecting a paycheck? A resounding *Yes!* There is a lot of luck in winning any tournament; this helps level the playing field. One tournament winner of the White Marlin Open told the story of how the crew had not caught a fish and had given up all hope. They were in the cabin playing cards when the tournament-winning white marlin committed suicide by eating a skirted ballyhoo off a long rigger. Of course, this is the exception. Knowing what you are doing increases the odds of luck occurring. And, knowing how the professionals fish just might increase those odds. What follows are some of the Pros' techniques.

The white marlin is the big-money fish when it comes to many offshore tournaments. The fish is famous for its aerial displays and ability to throw a hook!

The winning, big-money ticket in most tournaments has the title of billfish and this is where the pros concentrate efforts. They only pull a billfish spread behind transoms, even though many tournaments pay out money for many different qualifying species. There is something to be said for tournament fishing where an angler targets a species that has less competition. For example, the shark category in the White Marlin Open has less than a handful of anglers targeting them. Targeting shark or other species, like wahoo, during a billfish tournament greatly increases chances that prize money may end up in your pocket. However, since most anglers target billfish in these tournaments and that is where the big money payouts come from, that is what this chapter addresses.

There's no "correct" type of spread, bait, or way to troll for billfish; but, there *are* wrong ways to billfish. If your idea of participation in a billfish tournament includes sitting on the bridge, nodding off, and in general enjoying a couple relaxing days on the ocean with your buddies having a few drinks and a bunch of laughs, save your money or fish tuna tournaments where the fish hook themselves.

It can be tiring watching lines all day in a billfish tournament, but this is not the way to end up standing on the podium collecting a sizeable paycheck.

The Basic Billfish Spread

The following is a basic billfish spread and it works. It consists of a five-line spread, two teasers, and two dredges. Most professionals feel more lines do not increase chances of catching fish, but only complicates a bite. If billfish are hungry, they will rise to one of the presented baits. In addition, two pitch rods are rigged and ready with ballyhoo stored in tubes with saltwater to prevent them from drying out. After rigging pitch rod ballyhoo, they are water tested to assure swimming ability. Pitching a ballyhoo that spins to white marlin is a sure way to end the bite. If the boat does not have a bridge, adjust the following as necessary. Two teasers are run off the outriggers and controlled from the bridge or from the pit off teaser rods. Two dredges are run off riggers, placing them in clean water outside of prop turbulence. If riggers will not support the weight of dredges, they can be run off each corner of transom, but make sure they run under the turbulence from props clearly visible from below. Two flat line baits are set behind the dredges. Two rigger line baits are run within sight, with a fifth line run in the middle of the spread, bringing up the rear. This line catches the attention of any billfish, which is missed when setting the hook on any of the other lines or the bait-and-switch. Normally, this fifth line bait is set far enough to be out of sight, meaning any bite must be considered a billfish and, automatically, the reel is free-spooled for five seconds before sliding drag level up to apply pressure for the circle hook to set.

Billfishing requires 100 percent attention if success is to be achieved consistently. The number-one reason the same boats rise to the top of tournament boards and collect checks is that they fish like a well-oiled machine—doing the same thing over and over. The crew knows each other's moves, and lines are watched every minute of every tournament, from lines in to lines out of water at day's end.

Many teams assign one angler to each fishing rod. The angler does not leave the rod and is prepared whenever a marlin rises to the bait. Other teams attack with a different philosophy and have designated duties for each member in their area of expertise. One team member may be responsible for setting the hook, then hands off the rod to an angler whose expertise is fighting the fish (if rod handoff is allowed in the tournament). Another member is given the task of wiring the fish, measurement or gaffing, if necessary. One angler is often assigned the job of only controlling/watching teasers. Then, when a billfish becomes interested, this person retrieves the teaser for implementation of the bait-and-switch. Bottom line, everyone knows their jobs and works as part of the team. Does this guarantee success? No, but it goes a long way in upping chances that less mistakes are made. These teams do not get caught with feet flat on the deck—they stay on their toes.

Ballyhoo is the number-one bait for white marlin and sailfish, with mullet, mackerel, and squid popular behind transoms for blue marlin. Of course, artificial lures are used, but they are seldom mixed with natural bait for the pure billfisherman spread. (How to rig ballyhoo just like the pros is covered in Chapter 8: White Marlin.) There are several ways to rig ballyhoo on circle hooks, but the method in Chapter 8 is used by ninety percent of boats. Is it the only way that will catch fish? Absolutely not—just suffice it to say, rigged bait must look natural and swim correctly.

Thirty-pound class tackle is standard for whites, hatchets, spearfish, and sails with 80- to 100-pound leaders. Blue marlin requires at least 50 class tackle, with 80- or 130-pound class preferred, using 250- to 500-pound leaders. All leaders are wind-on to assist in wiring of fish.

How fast to troll? Speed is not regulated by the GPS or RPMs. That is a starting point, but depending on water conditions—like current, wind, and waves—boat speed changes. Observe bait and find a speed where the bait looks real and swims naturally. If heading into a 2-knot current and boat speed is shown as 5.5 knots over the bottom, in reality, the bait is swimming at 7.5 knots and probably skipping on the surface. This is fine, if that is your intended bait presentation. However, most rigged bait swim best between 3 and 6 knots.

Where to begin trolling? Best success comes when fishing good-looking water. (Not wanting to be redundant, read sub-section "Good Water" in Chapter 24: Burn a Hole. This explains what to look for and where lines should be dropped.)

At least one pitch rod is rigged and within hand's reach for the bait-and-switch when fish come up on teasers. Although many boats have two rods ready, one thirty-pound rig and another fifty or eighty-pound class, in case a blue marlin makes an appearance. Regardless of the number of rods or teasers that are behind the transom, invest in at least one dredge, preferably two.

Dredges

The importance of a dredge for billfishing cannot be overstated. A large dredge containing many baits representing a school of fish certainly draws attention, but do not discount any size dredge's ability to raise fish. Strip teaser, rubber fish, or natural bait dredges all work. A natural bait dredge (ballyhoo or mullet) is the first choice with a combination of natural and rubber bait following. (Chapter 8 explains how to rig ballyhoo for a dredge.)

Hooking Up

Watching the spread and observing a billfish before it attacks greatly increases hookup percentage. When a fish appears, take rod in hand, place reel in free-spool, hold bait in position with light thumb pressure, and turn the clicker off. If the clicker is left on as the fish spools line, its vibration and noise is transmitted through the line. Remember as a kid tying two paper cups together with a piece of string and how you could hear your friend on the other end talking? (Maybe I am dating myself.) Often, anglers do not associate the clicker as being the culprit that causes dropped bait.

Speaking of vibration and noise, when a billfish is raised, keep noise to a minimum. It is difficult not to yell, jump, or bang around the pit when a bite occurs. However, all that sound transmits loudly underwater. Ever stick your head underwater and hear a boat engine transmitting sound? If so, you get the point of hatches slamming and feet pounding around. But I've gotten off topic; getting back to the bite.

Point the rod at the fish, keeping slight thumb pressure on spool. Too much thumb pressure may result in the bait being ripped off the hook or pulled out of the fish's mouth. Once the bite is felt, begin free-spooling. The art of free-spooling allows fishing line to "fall" from the end of the rod tip. Very, very, very slight pressure is necessary to prevent backlashing, as the billfish swims off with the bait. The line being free-spooled leaves the reel naturally at a steady rate, caused from the boat's forward progress. Once the bait is picked up, line leaving the spool speeds up, indicating the fish is swimming off and swallowing the bait. Now count to five and slowly advance the drag lever while the rod is pointed towards the fish. This is an important step, so I'll reiterate: slowly advance the drag. This step assures the circle hook is not snatched out of the fish's mouth and gives time to set securely in the corner of the mouth. Once the weight of the fish is felt, slowly raise the rod tip and begin the battle. There is no need to "set" a circle hook. This only increases the size of the hole where the hook has penetrated.

Acquiring drop-back skill is obtained by actually having the opportunity to perform the move, time and time again. For anglers who do not have 100, fifty, or even twenty-five shots a year at billfish, they should run the hooking process through the mind over and over, until it becomes embedded. Then, when a bite occurs, the steps are executed flawlessly.

If the bite is a swing and miss, do not assume the billfish swam off. Often, the fish is still following below the spread out of sight, watching the baits. To entice another bite, immediately raise the rod tip high overhead and wind to get bait back on the surface. This move creates the illusion of bait fleeing and often provokes another bite. A few sharp jerks often helps in a second attack, giving another opportunity at a hookup. While that angler is trying to get the fish back on the bait, all the other anglers should have remaining rods in hand, ready and watching their bait, in case the fish switches to another rod. (These anglers should not be looking at the rod with the first bite!)

Bait-and-switch

The bait-and-switch takes teamwork to pull off, but surprisingly results in a good percentage of hook ups. When a billfish rises on a teaser, there is no time to waste. The teaser is immediately retrieved to the boat at a moderate, steady rate of speed; the billfish chases. While the teaser is retrieved, another angler drops pitch bait and places it in line with the teaser. The rod is pointed towards the fish with the reel in free-spool, clicker off, and enough thumb pressure to stop line from coming off the reel. The billfish normally switches over as the bait comes into view. If not, the teaser can be snatched away, leaving the rigged bait as the only choice. All this occurs in a matter of seconds, reiterating the importance of paying attention to the spread and reacting quickly. This leads back to the number-one reason professional billfish teams are successful. They are ready when a bite opportunity presents itself.

Now, go register for a tournament and win some money!

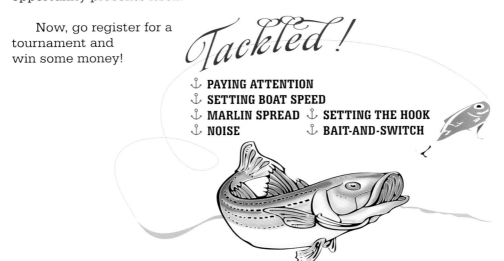

Tackled!

- PAYING ATTENTION
- SETTING BOAT SPEED
- MARLIN SPREAD — SETTING THE HOOK
- NOISE — BAIT-AND-SWITCH

Chapter 12
Listen!

Tips to prevent line separation

It was going to be a great-weather day offshore and the Fisherman was looking forward to the day's charter. As often happened, the charter booked a marlin/tuna trip through the marina office. The only information received was on the trip ticket, which included the name, address, and phone number of the person who booked and paid for the trip, along with the number of anglers in the party. The Fisherman enjoyed meeting anglers and also fishing for two different species. This broke up a day offshore, meaning the first half of the day would be spent trolling for marlin along the 100 fathom line and the other half chunkin for yellowfin tuna on one of the inner lumps. The yellowfin had been cooperative the previous few days and the Fisherman felt the charter should catch at least a couple, if not hang their fair share on the scale at day's end. There was not as much hope for marlin, since it was still early in summer and only a few had been raised, let alone caught.

Early the next morning, after quick introductions and storing gear below, lines were cast off and, once clearing the six-mile-an-hour buoy in the inlet, the boat came up onto plane, as the sun greeted everyone with a beautiful horizon to the east.

The plan was to run into the deep for billfish and troll back into the thirty-fathom lumps, and chunk during the afternoon when the tuna bite had been most productive recently, due to full moon. As mentioned, on a full moon, tuna feed all night and, with full stomachs, often take a break after the sun comes up.

The boat rode easily upon long, ten-second-interval swells, as the charter was asked questions and assessed for fishing ability. All the anglers had fresh-water experience, but little saltwater, and none for tuna or marlin. When trying to explain the workings of the reels and how important it was to let the drags do their jobs, one of the anglers injected that he had caught salmon in Alaska and was experienced in catching "BIG" fish.

The large-framed man's voice sounded as if a bear was growling when he spoke. Before the Fisherman could continue, the angler launched into telling a fishing story. As the Fisherman listened, he got the impression the man was, no doubt, an expert on any topic. Apparently, his buddies never heard the story and rather intently listened. It was apparent they gave him credit for being the most experienced member of the charter with nods and approving glances back and forth.

When Salmonman finished his story, the Fisherman delicately explained that catching salmon was nothing like having a marlin or tuna on the end of a fishing line. He finished explaining how to fight a fish by lifting the rod and retrieving line

A lone fisherman stands at the tip of the north jetty of the Ocean City, Maryland, inlet. He may not catch a fish, but the view certainly made climbing out of bed worth the effort.

with the reel, stressing how important it was to always remember to keep slack out of the line by beginning to wind before lowering the rod tip. Everyone listened with the exception of the Salmonman, who found it more interesting to look out over the ocean.

Seldom did the Fisherman meet someone he did not care for, but a feeling that this could become a long day crossed his mind. The charter was left to relax in the salon and the Fisherman returned to the pit to finish rigging lines.

Finally, the boat came off plane and marlin spread was set behind the transom.

"Who is catching the first fish?"

The charter looked at one another until Salmonman bellowed, "I'll show them how it's done!"

For the next couple hours, the boat trolled a temperature break and weed line that was beginning to form. It was a pain constantly winding in bait to remove seaweed picked up; however, the area was probably the best shot at catching a white this early in the year. Lines were pulled cross current, down current, and against current, all without so much as a nibble. Just as Salmonman was complaining to his buddies about no fish—as they often do—a white marlin appeared out of nowhere and was chasing a naked flat line split-bill rigged ballyhoo.

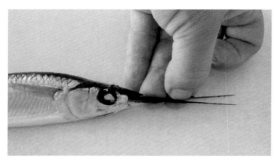

Ballyhoo bill is easily split in two with a fingernail. Rigging Split-bill ballyhoo creates bait that swims with a lot of action.

Rig a Split-bill ballyhoo just like a standard J-hook with exception that the leader is placed in middle of bill and rigging wire wraps bill back together.

The Fisherman picked rod up and free-spooled while silently counting to five before sliding the drag lever up. He felt the hook find its mark in the corner of the jaw and the rod doubled over with drag screaming.

Salmonman was already in the fighting chair with outstretched hands shouting, "Give me the rod!" just as the marlin came out of the water like a ballistic missile; it created a rainbow spray. Once the line came tight again, the rod was handed off and line continued screaming off the reel. The next three seconds went well.

Then Salmonman shouted, "There's too much drag!" and before the Fisherman could say anything or react, Salmonman pulled the drag lever back to the *off* position and rod straightened up! And, that fast, Salmonman was the holder of a new, world-record backlash.

The rod immediately doubled back over, followed by a loud snap, which sounded like a .22 rifle going off.

Salmonman looked up and proclaimed, "There's something wrong with this reel."

A fisherman's nightmare, not the tangle…the lost white marlin!

It took all the control he could muster, but the Fisherman bit his lip and remained silent. The next hour did not produce any more action and the boat picked up lines and ran the last few miles to where tuna were being caught. Trolling rods were exchanged for standup 50 class International outfits for chunkin, as the anchor headed towards bottom. Several dozen boats were set up on the popular lump. Scanning the horizon, the bite was on and several anglers could be observed hooked up. Fifteen minutes later, the line being handfed (see Chapter 7 for chunking techniques) was snatched from the Fisherman's fingers. The rod bent over and drag screamed.

Before the Fisherman could say a word, Salmonman shouted, "Give me the rod."

As the rod was handed off, the Fisherman said with a stern voice, "Do not touch the drag!"

The yellowfin had a good head of steam and spooling line quickly, but not for long. Salmonman placed his thumb on the spool and, at the same time, shouted, "OUCH!"

Once again, a .22 rifle went off as rod came upright! Salmonman had totally missed the morning speech on letting a drag do its job. The only good to come out of the whole ordeal that the Fisherman could tell was the blister forming on Salmonman's thumb, which was being soothed in his mouth. Salmonman mumbled something about it was still his turn as the Fisherman instructed one of the anglers to keep throwing chunks since fish were behind the transom. Lines were reset.

In the next ten minutes, two more fish were hooked and Salmonman managed to lose both. One changed direction and charged the boat, creating slack in the line. When line went slack, Salmonman proclaimed, "He's gone," and released his tight grip on the rod. The Fisherman luckily grabbed the rod and saved it from the depth of the ocean, just as the line came tight again before snapping. Salmonman had also missed that part of the morning conversation about winding as quickly as possible when you think a fish is lost. He snapped the other tuna off when rearing back hard to "set the hook again," as he put it.

The Fisherman could see on his buddies' faces that they had had enough—which was nothing compared to the Fisherman's thoughts on the situation. The Fisherman told another angler to put on the belt and harness. The remaining three anglers managed to each catch a tuna before calling it a day.

At one point, Salmonman spoke up and started to offer advice to his one buddy when the tuna sounded down under the boat. The Fisherman turned around and flashed a glance; Salmonman's words trailed off to silence. The Fisherman then explained to the angler to bend over and put the rod down as deep as possible, so the line did not tangle and snap off on the strut or prop. Once the tuna swam back out from under the boat, the fight was back on and it was eventually gaffed.

The Fisherman was glad to get back on the dock—very glad!

As the three tuna were being offloaded for cleaning, Salmonman looked at the Fisherman and got as far as "Hey—" when his one buddy interrupted, looking him square in the eyes, and said, "Shut the hell up!"

Tackled!

⚓ **TRUST REEL'S DRAG**
⚓ **SLACK LINE**

Chapter 13

Bluefin

Drift chunkin for bluefin

Bluefin tuna. They don't obtain the name of "giant" for nothing. The bluefin is the largest member of the tuna family. Four-year-olds are eighty to ninety pounds; let another year pass and they give most anglers more than they can handle on rod and reel, pulling scales down to near 150 pounds—certainly true eating machines that put on pounds quickly. They are capable of reaching 500 pounds by age ten, and one-half ton by their seventeenth year. The commercial market value for bluefin has skyrocketed beyond imagination, with one bluefin receiving 1.76 million dollars after receiving the highest grade possible. Yeah, *one* bluefin! That worked out to $3,600 per pound at a market in Tokyo, although market price normally is closer to $15 per pound. Recreational fishermen cannot sell bluefin without a license, but punish themselves by targeting the fish purely for its pleasure on the palate and attempting to whip them into submission—no one ever accused anglers of being smart. Bluefin definitely are a test of man against beast.

Just as the Fisherman was finishing up dinner one Wednesday evening, the phone rang.

"Want to go fishing?"

It was a fishing buddy whose son and daughter-in-law had just arrived in town for vacation. Neither had ever gone toe-to-toe with a tuna and wanted the chance to tangle with one. With a favorable weather forecast for that Friday, the trip was set.

Chasing bluefin seemed like the right move, since the friend's son loved sushi. And after the excellent bluefin bite the Fisherman experienced the day before while chunking on a twenty-fathom lump, it certainly seemed like a great choice for a day offshore. With room still on the boat, the Fisherman's brother-in-law joined in for the trip as well.

Thursday evening, a captain called to say he'd had a great day, slammed a dozen yellowfin, and raised a couple whites in Washington Canyon. He went on to say the deep bite really turned on and everyone working the 100-fathom tip had a good day. There were even a few bigeye and a blue marlin caught by the charter fleet. The information was certainly appreciated, although the Fisherman knew it was actually a little salt being rubbed in the wound, since both his feet had been on dry land that day.

With the new, updated fishing information, there were thoughts of changing plans regarding where to run the next morning. He called his friend and discussed options but, finally, the original plan of attack stayed intact. Too many times

The Fisherman believes one of the best parts of chartering is sunrise.

second guessing and changing the direction on the compass ended up with a dismal-looking killbox at day's end.

Next morning, at 4:30 a.m., the boat cleared the inlet with bluefin in the cross-hairs. The Fisherman was not a fan of running in the dark, but wanted to catch the early bite if one developed, as it often did. Flat, calm sea's allowed the miles to fly by and, soon, the crew was greeted to a beautiful sunrise, bringing with it the promise of a great day.

The boat slowed and moved along an edge as a watchful eye was kept upon the sonar. A few large marks appeared, indicating possible bluefin as the boat approached the southwest corner of a lump known as the Hambone.

There are two ways to chunk for bluefin: on the hook (anchor) or drift. While both methods are productive, one of the key factors in determining which strategy to use is not having the bait spin in the current. When little to no current is present, the Fisherman preferred anchoring. This allowed chunks to be thrown over to form a chunk line behind the boat to draw in the tuna. While chunks are still thrown over while drifting, between boat drift and current, the chunks end up widespread and, to his way of thinking, possibly not as productive. Also, when on the hook, a school of tuna could be kept behind the transom as long as chunk was thrown—meaning several fish from a school often could be caught. This seemed more difficult while drifting. Although, in a strong current, drifting really is the best option.

The Fisherman decided to give it a shot, after seeing a few more marks and the anchor headed towards bottom. Rods were set and the crew began chunkin (for chunkin techniques, see Chapter 7).

Over the next hour, a couple fish were observed caught out of the handful of boats on the horizon. However, under their boat, the sonar showed the fish had pulled a "Houdini" and disappeared. With current falling off and chunks falling straight towards the bottom, the Fisherman decided to pull anchor and run a couple miles to the Northeast corner where a cluster of boats were forming. Upon arrival at the new location, with no wind and hardly any current, for some reason, all the boats were drifting. The Fisherman certainly had the option of anchoring, but when a fleet of boats are drifting and one captain anchors in the middle, he can expect to find other captains not happy with the decision.

The Fisherman began drifting with the fleet. The bluefin were hungry and several boats had bent rods. Fifteen minutes later, several fish showed on the sonar eating chunks being thrown and a drag screamed. Being the first fish of the day, the daughter-in-law was given the honor. She had been prepared for battle with the harness and belt already adjusted. In addition, the workings of the reel, how to handle the rod, and what to do during blistering runs had already been gone over. She was ready for standup action.

A fighting chair is ideal for trolling. But when chunkin for either yellowfin or bluefin while drifting in a fleet, the boat must constantly maneuver to stay on top of the fish to avoid line cut off. Other captains often try to assist by moving their boats when possible, since boats fish in closer proximity than when anchored. But a couple hundred yards of line stretched out is a recipe for disaster. The girl listened, keeping good pressure on the fish as the boat moved within the fleet. By standing upright, with back straight, the girl avoided lower back pain, one of the main reasons bluefin whip many anglers into submission, instead of the other way around. Over the next forty-five minutes, she did an awesome job working the tuna while the boat chased the fish over a half mile. Finally, the tuna tired, at which point it circled within sight under the boat. This is normal tuna procedure when tired and where many anglers find it difficult to make headway retrieving line. The trick to bringing a bluefin to gaff is, as the fish swims away from the boat and reaches the top of the arch, rod tip must be held fairly high with good pressure. Line is retrieved as tuna circles back towards the boat, but the tuna's head must be kept upwards with pressure. If done properly, on each circle the tuna rises a few inches. The Fisherman watched the girl accomplish what many of her counterparts had been unable to do over the years of chartering and finally managed to get the fish within a gaff shot. Shortly thereafter, her first bluefin hit the deck.

Once blood was washed off the deck and gear squared away, the boat ran back south and set up with the fleet for another drift. It did not take long until the

Tuna Tip

Often, anglers do not gut tuna caught, due to wanting an accurate weight on the scale at day's end. Icing down tuna without gutting does not cool off the meat quickly and detracts from flavor. Unless fishing a tournament, a tuna should always be dressed and the body cavity packed with ice. This small step will be appreciated on the dinner table much more than those extra pounds showing on the scale.

This young lady put on a clinic instructing how to land a bluefin tuna on standup gear.

friend's son got into a brawl. The fish had some spunk and, after a half hour, the scorecard was about even. Since this rod presented bait near the surface, it had thirty-pound fluorocarbon leader. A limited amount of pressure could be applied. Tuna often are leader shy in bright sunlight and dropping down in leader size often results in bites. As an hour approached, the stubborn fish took the lead and inflicted serious lower back pain on the man. The Fisherman's buddy took over the rod and finished pumping the tuna to the surface. With the limit of bluefin already in the killbox, the hook was removed and the tuna swam away, none the worst for wear, as a couple very tired anglers managed smiles.

Next drift, the deep rod went off. This rod had fifty-pound leader and it was a good thing, since it was the largest fish of the day. The Fisherman's brother-in-law put on a clinic of how to handle a bluefin on stand-up gear. He was able to best the beast, well over 100 pounds, in about thirty minutes.

As the tuna swam away, the Fisherman inquired as to who was ready for another bluefin. However, there were no takers from the four tired anglers. If a yellowfin bite had developed, the crew might have found the energy to catch a couple more; but, instead, they decided to save remaining arm strength for a little wreck fishing. The Fisherman ran just inside the twenty-fathom line to one of the many popular wrecks that provided rich bottom habitat. Sea bass were stacked up, drop after drop—double headers came over the gunwale.

Finally, everyone was satisfied with the look of the killbox and the boat. Shortly thereafter, it was up on plane heading for port. After the boat was clean, as the sun set in the western sky, the task of butchering the bluefin began. Fresh sushi was being consumed almost at the rate the fish was being butchered! Everyone commented that it was the best they'd ever had the pleasure to eat— this, no doubt, from preserving the flavor by being bled out, gutted, and packing the stomach with ice right after hitting the deck.

Put the Fish in the Boat

Here are a few tips when chunkin for tuna to help put them on deck.

- ⚓ **Being spooled?** Back off the drag and reduce pressure. Many times this will slow down or turn a fish.

- ⚓ **Chase the fish to retrieve line faster.** Run a twenty- to thirty-degree angle to the fish, instead of backing down to retrieve line.

- ⚓ **Watch the reel.** If line is lost every time the rod is lifted, lift slower to prevent drag slippage and allow line retrieval.

- ⚓ **When a fish sounds, move the boat to maintain a good fighting angle.**

- ⚓ **Constant pressure wears a fish down.** Fishing is work. Stay in shape!

The Fisherman prepares to release a "Ben Franklin" bluefin. Notice two eight-ounce egg sinkers with rubber band used to keep bait near bottom. (Chapter 7 explains this rigging technique.)

Catching sea bass finished off another great day on the ocean.

Chapter 14
Balls of Fun

Technique for bailing mahi mahi off lobster balls

Riddle: Nature's perfection can be observed no better than this fish that has the ability to reproduce at eight inches of length, which is obtained after only four or five months of age. Their ferocious appetite allows rapid growth, achieving a length of forty-five inches by two years of age, with an average life span of about four years. They're extremely plentiful, excellent table fair, and one of the most beautiful fish that swims the ocean. If that's not enough, they are not picky eaters and devour just about anything that comes in their path after being enticed. Now, if that's not the perfect game fish I would like to know which is!

Just about anything floating provides a haven for these fish that anglers call mahi mahi, dolphin, dorado, or *Coryhaena hippurus* (if you hang around with marine biologists). As early summer waters warm, they first take up residence around commercial lobster and sea bass pot floats found in the deep. As summer progresses and waters warm further, the fish move closer inshore. They are often even found around floating structures within sight of land in the mid-Atlantic.

The most productive floats are those that have been in the water for some time and that have developed growth. This in turn attracts marine life, which in turn attracts small fish, which…well, you get the point of a food chain. There's probably not a more aggressive pelagic swimming, nor one that can be counted on to consistently provide anglers with action, once water temperatures reach the low seventies.

Trolling certainly is a popular method of catching mahi and will be covered in Chapter 19. But, for the present time, let us take a look at what is commonly called bailing dolphin. Success comes down to being prepared. Once action begins, it is not the time to cut bait, tie hooks, or search for pliers, etc. Spinning or light casting tackle in the twelve- to twenty-pound class handles the chore. Having a couple extra rods rigged and ready to go is a real time saver. For real efficiency, designate someone as the mate. This poor angler gets to remove hooks, bait rods, retie hooks and leaders, net/gaff fish, and listen to his buddies screaming in his ears with excitement. But, this person keeps everyone catching fish!

Plan ahead on how many pounds of fish are to be kept and then keep count. Federal regulations currently allot ten fish per angler. However, with a half-dozen anglers throwing fish in the killbox, numbers add up in a short time. In addition, when fish run six, eight, or ten pounds, a tremendous amount of meat can be caught.

Very few pelagic are as beautiful as the mahi. Always keep one hooked fish in the water and others will hang around, as demonstrated by this mahi following a hooked fish.

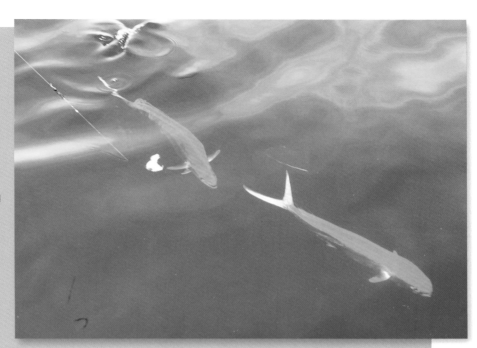

Keeping the rod tip low to the water helps prevent mahi from going airborne as often and throwing the hook.

Think conservation—this is one fishery that is not in trouble; let's keep it that way.

Smaller fish can be swung over the gunwales. This does not mean lifting straight up out of the water, which is when a lot of fish find the ability to unhook themselves, falling back into the ocean and causing words not found in Webster's to be uttered. However, by pulling the fish horizontally through water, before creating an angle upwards over the gunwale, most fish will be landed. The idea is not to snatch the fish out of the water, but gently swing. Gaffers are fish over ten pounds and, as the name implies, need to be gaffed. A two- or three-inch head being the weapon of choice helps prevent the thin mahi body from slipping through the head of the gaff.

Then there are those fish that are just a little too large to swing over the gunwale, but not large enough to gaff. This is when a net comes in handy. Often, offshore anglers fishing for pelagic don't think of landing fish with a net. But this is one occasion where carrying one onboard will save a lot of fish.

How does an angler get to the point of using a gaff or net? Easy; slowly ride by any floating debris and look underneath with a good pair of polarized sunglasses to observe fish. If observed, cast baited lines to their vicinity. Dolphin can be a slow starter, rushing out from undercover only to look at the bait and swim back to the shade. If fish are shy taking the hook, throw a small handful of bait to get them feeding; this can consist of cut-up pieces of fish, squid, butterfish, etc. Concealing the hook and using fluorocarbon helps to turn on a bite as well. Artificial lures can be used with success at times, casting around the floating object. However, cut bait is more productive. Even if fish are not observed under floating debris, sometimes they are suspended at depths out of sight. A handful of bait thrown near the flotsam will raise the fish to the surface, if there.

Once a dolphin is hooked, keep the fish in the water until a second is hooked up. Do not land the first fish until another has been hooked. A school normally will not leave the area when a hooked fish is left in the water. I cannot over emphasize this point:

ALWAYS KEEP ONE HOOKED DOLPHIN IN THE WATER!

When action slows and fish get finicky with one type of bait, changing to a different offering often turns the bite back on. When fish are in a feeding frenzy, as the boat drifts away from the floating object, the fish will follow as long as one remains in the water. If working lobster balls (floats), when action ceases, seek out other balls close by. This gives the fish time to swim back and regroup. Often, anglers can use three or four balls in a given area and literally catch fish for hours.

A trick that always turns on the bite is carrying live minnows onboard. A live well is ideal for this or a cooler works with a few pieces of ice and no water. The minnows will live all day. A few minnows thrown in the area of tight-lipped mahi is almost a guarantee that mouths open and chomp at anglers' bait!

One of the attractive aspects of mahi that anglers find appealing is their acrobatic ability.

Florescent colors glistening in sunlight is a wonder of nature and pleasant to an angler's eye, but it also increases chances of a thrown hook. It is a natural reaction to raise the rod tip when the fish comes out of the water to reduce slack. However, as soon as slack is removed, winding and lowering the rod tip near the surface of the water will help keep your dinner under water, increasing chances of another fish in the killbox.

The Fisherman's wife with gaffer mahi caught bailing.

A net is essential for mahi too large to swing over gunnel, but still a little small to gaff.

Bailing dolphin is a great "Plan B" when trolling does not produce. It has often saved the day for many a charter for captains. Marlin and tuna may be at the top of the list when pulling out of the slip, but a batch of good eating like this helps to ease the pain of no tuna steaks!

Notice high flyer in background. It is always worth trolling by these; if mahi are caught, the decision can be made whether to stop and bail.

Tackled!

- ⚓ **PREPARATION**
- ⚓ **LANDING**
- ⚓ **BAIT**
- ⚓ **KEEP HOOKED FISH IN WATER**

A nice batch of bailed mahi like this has saved many trips offshore when fishing is slow. A couple deep drops on this day added red rosies as well.

Chapter 15
Ocean Stripers

Trolling for striped bass in fall/winter

Four hundred and forty-four miles north of the head waters of the Chesapeake Bay, in Cooperstown, New York, water from Lake Otsego begins to flow downstream to form the Susquehanna River. It traverses small communities nestled in picturesque valleys, woods, rural countryside, and bustling metropolitan cities in the states of New York, Pennsylvania, and Maryland, while en route to the Conowingo Dam, located near Port Deposit, Maryland. Here, chilly spring water rushes over spillways before slowing a couple miles downstream. Boulders and rocks warmed in spring's sun transfer heat to the water before finally mixing with the salinity water of the Chesapeake Bay in an area known as the Susquehanna flats, near Havre De Grace, Maryland, where the famed Chesapeake Bay begins. Largemouth bass, white perch, yellow perch, herring, shad, and a host of other species call this home for spawning each spring. The importance of this marine nursery cannot be overstated, especially for striped bass, whose offspring from this location swims the whole East Coast of the United States.

The cold of late fall is worth enduring as the Fisherman's son and nephew show.

For the past ten years, she made the migration back to the area where she was conceived, not knowing why, but swimming by a mystical internal compass. Somehow, the eighteen-year-old female had avoided gill nets, which at times seemed to stretch from the Eastern to Western shores of the Chesapeake. This year, a class of male stripers hatched in 2004 came of breeding age for the first time and returned to their place of birth. It would be the first of many yearly migrations for those who escaped fishermen's hooks and nets. The males had been present for a couple weeks, swimming about and feeding on the Susquehanna flats, waiting on egg-laden females to make an appearance to continue the circle of life. As the big female made her way into the breeding area, she sensed water temperatures nearing fifty-five degrees and nature instinctively told her it was time. Millions of eggs dropped from the female as several males turned the water a milky color and eggs were fertilized. With her task completed, a couple quick tail flips propelled her south towards the ocean, 200 miles away.

It was no coincidence schools of menhaden invaded the Chesapeake Bay this time as well and she fed until her stomach budged—day after day replenishing energy used to spawn. She momentarily stopped for a few days, near the Chesapeake Bay Tunnel [a twenty-three-mile marvel of man's innovation built in 1964 at the sum of 200 million dollars]. But all she knew was that the concrete pilings and rocks provided rips and currents in rushing tides that confused baitfish, creating easy meals. Finally entering the Atlantic Ocean, she turned north and, for the next month, swam past the coastlines of Maryland, Delaware, and New Jersey, until arriving at an area fishermen called Montauk, New York. For the rest of summer, this was home and she feasted upon the delicacies of the ocean caught up in swirling water around jetties. Another inch in length was obtained over summer and now she weighed close to fifty pounds. Northern wind finally swept down and ended summer's reign, giving way to fall and, impulsively, she began another journey: south to winter off the coast of North Carolina, joining millions of other striped bass migrating to do the same.

"Hey, want to try for stripers tomorrow? Captain Ron called with rumor that fish were caught this morning just off the beach in front of the radio tower."

It was news the Fisherman and his cousin had been waiting to hear. Crabbing and summer charter season were long gone. Flounder fishing had been decent until the water cooled a month earlier, driving the flat, odd-looking fish into the deep offshore. Since then, toggin around the jetties with green crabs passed fishing time while waiting on the arrival of striped bass from up north. Migrating striped bass in late fall/early winter was the last fishery the Fisherman enjoyed before rods were cleaned and carefully stored away for the coming year.

With the striped bass rumor, the Fisherman had called his cousin. Next morning, the boat eased out the inlet and turned north for a short, three-mile run to a shoal a couple miles off the beach for the first striper trip of the winter.

Ocean trolling for striped bass, while not new, gained popularity in the mid-Atlantic over the past few years, once charter boat captains realized there was enough interest in the fishery to extend charter season. Depending on weather/water temperatures, stripers could be caught until the beginning of January. (No, the ocean is not a pleasant place when cold wind howls out of the Northeast and temperatures plummet to sub-freezing. But mixed in, are beautiful calm days of early winter—perfect for catching a few stripers to give avid anglers a fix to get them through the upcoming doldrums of a long, blistery, winter, deep freeze.)

Trolling for ocean stripers uses the same technique as trolling in the Chesapeake Bay for spring rock (see Chapter 10 for technique tips).

"Ready to set lines?"

"Yeah!"

The throttles were pulled back and the Fisherman watched, as lures disappeared into the ocean in search of the first striper of winter.

Striper fishing in the ocean can often be easy, due to the fact gannets and gulls congregate over the stripers feeding on baitfish. A good pair of binoculars locates birds, and running to those locations and trolling under the birds normally produces fish. When the fish are thick, casting lures can be productive as well. However, on this day, no birds were within sight and efforts would be directed at trolling along shoal edges, where baitfish often congregate with stripers close in tow.

It did not take long until a rod bent over and, shortly thereafter, the net was slid under what was to become many dinners.

A couple more passes and a double header came over the gunwales.

Needing one more fish for their limit, the bow was pointed towards a few birds that had begun working a half-mile south. However, the tandem rigged bucktails dragging behind the transom never got that far. A rod doubled over and drag screamed under the stress being applied from weight at the end of the line. Once the rod was in hand and the size of fish assessed, the Fisherman suggested that his cousin clear the rest of the lines. The Fisherman was careful not to put too much pressure on the fish and, after twenty minutes, a striped bass, unlike any the Fisherman had seen before, broke water with its bucket-sized mouth wide open in the boat wash. The bucktail was clearly visible, barely hooked in the corner of the mouth.

"Be careful...easy...take it easy with that leader!"

Slowly, hand over hand, the leader was retrieved as the exhausted fish grew closer to the net—fifteen feet, thirteen feet, eight feet—then, with enough energy for one last flip of its large powerful tail, the fish dislodged the fragile hold of the bucktail! The striper momentarily hung stationary on the surface before sinking from sight as the boat slowly continued forward. The Fisherman looked at his cousin, who stood at transom with leader in hand and mouth agape.

The corners of the Fisherman's mouth slowly curved upwards into a grin, "How big do you think she was?"

The cousin was speechless and just shook his head.

Under the surface, the big female quickly gained back strength and, within minutes, blended back in with other stripers on their journey south where they would spend winter on the continental shelf until nature said to swim north, back up the Chesapeake Bay, in spring to continue populating the species.

The Fisherman with the first striper of the fall/winter season; notice in the background how close to shore the fish often migrate.

The Fisherman's cousin with a double header, leaving one more fish necessary to fill daily quota.

Chapter 16
Winter

Fishing and physics

The jet stream reached down into southern Alabama and sucked in moist warm air from the Gulf of Mexico before making a sharp U-turn back northward along the eastern seaboard. The energized air currents barreled northward until running into a stationary cold front just north of the Outer Banks of North Carolina where, during summer, boats trolled for marlin and dolphin. Out here, on the edge of the canyons, warm Gulf Stream water collided with cold inshore waters, wind started circling counterclockwise, and, overnight, a deep low pressure system developed. While similar in aspect to a hurricane, this was commonly referred to as a nor'easter and took on a life of its own. Being on the cold side of the front, the Delmarva Peninsula was the battleground for weather supremacy. Overnight, winds increased to near fifty MPH out of the northeast, piling up heavy, wet snow.

The snow swirled in the door as the Fisherman closed it and stamped feet removing snow from boots.

"How long is it going to last?" The Fisherman's wife always said he could forecast weather better than men standing in front of TV cameras on the evening news. Spending day after day on the ocean, studying weather and trying to decide what conditions were going to be like was just part of chartering.

"System is being blocked from a high to the east; probably snow hard all day."

Close to a foot of snow fell overnight and the Fisherman just finished plowing out their 800-foot driveway on the farm. It would need to be done at least one more time, if not two, depending on snow accumulations. There really wasn't any hurry; it would be lucky if their back-country road got plowed within twenty-four hours. But the Fisherman always liked staying ahead of the rare snowstorms. Outside, the wind howled as the Fisherman paced back and forth like a wild, caged animal.

"There is nothing you can do; why don't you go clean your desk?" suggested his wife.

The desk was the collection area for the Fisherman. Egg sinkers pulled out of pocket at day's end, along with rusty hooks and old swivels found their way there. Scrap pieces of paper with scribbling of GPS numbers waiting to be written down in a logbook were mixed in with favorite books and important documents. Shelves full of fishing and hunting magazines, with articles to be read and interesting stories to be reread, all were stacked up. Shotgun shells, change, pens that didn't write, paper clips, and many other odds and ends were tucked into every cubby hole.

The desk was an ongoing joke; the Fisherman's wife never touched anything on the desk as it "might get lost!" And while it was true the Fisherman really didn't know what was under the piles of mess, if he was looking for something, this is where it was sure to be...somewhere!

Pretty rare to see this much snow on the
Eastern Shore of Maryland.

"Yeah, might as well, won't plow again for a couple hours."

He sat down and, one by one, started going through papers in the first pile. He really wasn't cleaning as much as organizing and relocating papers neatly from one side of the desk to the other—could never bring himself to throw anything away. Halfway through the first pile, he came across a notebook from high school physics class. When the book was discovered a year earlier in the attic, it had been placed on the desk as a reminder to use the topic for a magazine article. As he flipped through the pages, memories of senior year flooded his mind as if it was yesterday. Back then, as far as the Fisherman was concerned, school took up valuable fishing time. When spring's spawning fish were eager towards a hook, tardy absences were a weekly occurrence. His parents knew about this lack of good judgment whenever fish were brought home after school. But they ignored the missing of classes as long as grades were kept up.

The Fisherman leaned back in his chair and looked out the sliding-glass door, deep in thought—but didn't see the driving snow. Once again, he and his cousin were seventeen years young out on the back Bay fishing in the skiff. It was a beautiful, calm, spring morning and gulls filled ears with squawking sounds whenever silversides were driven to the surface by a school of hungry bluefish. It was run and gun fishing, chasing the gulls, and casting bucktails and small spoons to the snappers—catching two or three at each stop before the school sounded and popped up 100 yards away. Then there were those perfect mornings when incoming tide occurred right at daybreak. Instead of sitting in first period class, the Fisherman had spinning rod in hand, slowly drifting the swirling clear, clean water along the south jetty wall. The flounder were more than cooperative and inhaled the minnow/squid offerings. One morning, the bite was nonstop with net slipping under fish after fish that would never get the opportunity to spend summer in the back Bay. The side door by the gym was used to sneak back into school just in time for third-period class. Outside, on the school parking lot, in the bed of the pickup were a dozen flounder iced down in a cooler.

The Fisherman reminisced about trip after fishing trip before finally glancing back down at the book and realizing he never missed last-period class, which was physics. A grin crossed his face; the only reason he never missed this class was due to sitting next to Angela. The best part of senior year by far was sitting next to the senior class's prettiest girl. Angela could be described as the type of girl who made it extremely difficult for a guy to keep his mind on the right subject and certainly made it difficult to learn. Nonetheless, even with her distractions, a few things the teacher said must have sunk in. As he flipped through the book, written on one page...

Meaning of Force: a push or pull upon an object resulting from the object's interaction with another object.

The Fisherman smiled. This had nothing to do with Angela's good looks; however...he had scribbled it down anyway! Now, years later, he realized this rule explained how a fish could swim. This is why he signed up for physics—to learn usable information. Well, that and he'd heard that Angela was taking the course. Apparently, the teacher was unaware how important this information could be. Never did she mention the word "fish" one time in class.

For simplicity sake, a fish uses its fins to push water backwards. But a push on the water only serves to accelerate the water. In turn, the water reacts by pushing the fish forward, propelling the fish. The size of the force on the water equals the size of the force on the fish; the direction of the force on the water (backwards) is opposite to the direction of the force on the fish (forwards). For every action, there is an equal (in size) and opposite (in direction) reaction force. Action-reaction force pairs make it possible for fish to swim. This is commonly known as Newton's third law of motion.

Also found stuck between the pages in the notebook was his final term paper, across the front written: Good luck fishing! C+

The assignment was to explain force in your words. The Fisherman had written...

Tensional force: Tension is force transmitted through fishing line when pulled tight by a fish at one end and you on the other. Tensional force is directed along the line equally. However, when force exceeds fishing line strength, the line breaks. This is why fishing reels have drags.

He leaned back in the chair and thoughts went back to Angela with her long, flowing blond hair, beautiful smile, and the crush he'd had on her. It seemed impossible, but she actually paid less attention to the Fisherman than he did to the teacher. Now, forty-five years after physics class, once again Angela was consuming his thoughts. Consuming thoughts until...

"Your desk looks the same; what have you been doing in here? Thought you were going to plow again?"

The Fisherman snapped back to reality and looked outside at the new six inches of fallen snow. "Uhmm, been thinking about fishing. Was just getting ready to go out!"

Chapter 17

Toggin' Around

Advice for catching tautog

Only a mother could love a face like that! Yep, that pretty much sums up a tog, tautog, or blackfish—depending where you drop a line. But what this fish lacks in looks surely is made up for on the end of a line. Without a doubt, the slow-growing tog is one of the more difficult fish to hook and even more difficult to entice out of the structure it calls home. They invade inshore waters of the northeast in spring from Nova Scotia to South Carolina to spawn when water temperatures struggle to reach a balmy forty-five degrees. Popularity could be due to being one of the first fish available for anglers to pursue after being cooped up all winter reading fishing magazines or because they are such a challenge to hook—not to mention they rank high on the dinner plate.

In early spring, fish can be found close to shore around jetties, breakwaters, piers, and bridge abutments. As inshore waters warm, the fish move further offshore, taking up residence around bottom structures where water temperatures are more to their liking. These fish are not pelagic in nature and, once taking up residence on a piece of structure, often remain in close proximity throughout the summer and fall, before retreating back to their winter bailiwick. Because of this, it is possible to fish out a location and it is also why toggers spread out pressure and keep prime pieces of structure wrapped under a blanket of secrecy.

Anglers often are not too particular when it comes to what type fish is tugging on the end of their line. But, sooner or later, each finds him/herself drawn towards a specific species. For many of us, the addiction of pursuing and catching a certain type of fish consumes most fishing opportunities. And the passion for tog is no more evident than that of the Fisherman's uncle and father-in-law. Yellowfin could be thick offshore on the lumps. The Fisherman would invite them on open charter dates for a day offshore, but more often than not, they declined, choosing to go toggin. Their obsession to catch tog turns back the hands of time many decades. If there is a secret to catching this small-mouthed fish with big teeth, these two toggers had it down to a science. The Fisherman logged many hours over the years waiting on the signature *tap tap* bite of tog and considered himself a right-decent togger. However, when fishing with "the toggin team"…well, let's just say the Fisherman seldom caught his fair share!

"Hey Pop, looks nice tomorrow; you and Uncle want to try for the first flounder of the year?"

"Naw, going toggin; got room for ya."

And so logistics were discussed and, the next morning, the Fisherman was on his Uncle's Wellcraft headed to a wreck offshore.

Fishing the correct location is necessary when pursuing any fish. One of the most important factors in being successful is understanding where fish are located. It is a start to know tog-like structure, such as rock jetties or concrete bridge piling, which provide an environment where crabs, mussels, and shellfish attract them, or to fish rocky bottoms, ledges, or wrecks offshore.

But anglers must also learn where the fish congregate on the structure. The key to achieving bites is placing bait where fish are around or within the structure. It is not uncommon, when anchored over a wreck, only to have one angler catch the majority of the fish. Why? Their bait constantly falls within the wreck or in front of a hole or crack in the hull where fish are congregated. The fish are not very fond of swimming around the structure looking for a meal. Instead, they wait on the meal to find them. This leaves novice tog anglers often scratching their heads when watching other anglers catch fish, when they do not get a nibble.

As a Dive Master, the Fisherman saw it firsthand while scuba diving and spearfishing tog, time and time again. Tog like to hide back in the darkness or shadows of a wreck's deteriorating hull. They face outwards from their hiding locations where unsuspecting prey can be ambushed. Seldom were large tog ever found swimming very far from the cover of structure. Because of this, when anchored over a wreck, taking in or letting out a few feet of anchor line can make all the difference between success and failure. The same is true for moving the boat a few feet to one side or the other by changing where the anchor line rides off the bow cleat. At the very least, just moving your location on the boat to drop down a line makes a difference.

Depending on the size of structure, a wreck anchor is often the best choice. Wreck anchors offer an alternative to conventional anchoring. They can hold the boat almost directly over the wreck, easing the anchoring process. The anchors are easily made by welding ¼-inch rod for smaller boats or ⅜-inch for larger vessels. When finished fishing, the anchor line is secured to transom cleat and straightens out under power to be retrieved.

For the utmost in boat positioning, setting two anchors in a "V" shape assist in moving the boat around a wreck in order to find the most productive area. Drop a float on the wreck or structure when initially found. Ride around the float watching the depth finder display the wreck and learn in what direction it lays on the bottom, which areas have the most structure, and where sonar shows fish are congregated in relationship. In short, learn where you fish. Take the current and wind into consideration before setting the anchor to position the boat in the correct location over the fish. When encountering throwbacks coming over the side of the boat, first explore other areas of the structure for larger fish. If efforts do not return positive results, only then it is time to move on in search of a new wreck/structure.

To illustrate how important anchoring is, the Fisherman often spearfished tog at a popular wreck called the *African Queen* (38-08.366 74-52.624). The wreck is located about ten miles from the inlet at Ocean City, Maryland. During a violent storm, on December 30, 1958, the 590-foot steam-powered tanker ran aground, breaking in half. The stern section was refloated and towed to shore. But the bow section went to the bottom in about sixty-eight feet of water. One side of the upsidedown hull is sanded and pretty much void of life, while the other side looks like an aquarium, full of sea bass, triggerfish, ocean perch, tog, and flounder lying close to the hull. Again, understanding where fish are located is important. Set up on the wrong area of the wreck and it could be a very long, unproductive day.

On this particular morning, the Fisherman and two expert toggers set two anchors and, beneath them, laid the remains of the once proud Norwegian ship, the *African Queen*.

"Dollar on the first keeper?"

It was normal procedure for the bet to occur. The Fisherman should have just handed over the dollar bill right then and there, since he seldom won. Taking care of the anchoring chore fell upon him and assured he would be last getting bait in the

Tog are equipped with a set of choppers for crushing crab.

The Fisherman's father-in-law displays a wreck anchor. The rebar straightens out under pressure to release hold on the wreck. The anchor is bent back into shape and ready for next trip.

The Fisherman's uncle with first tog of the day; notice float in background marking wreck, this makes anchoring in correct location an easier process.

water. This day was no different—as he baited hook for first drop, his uncle had already swung the first keeper of the day on deck.

The KISS (*keep-it-simple-stupid*) system works best for toggin. Since the objective is to place bait within the structure, it goes without saying that snags are the order of the day. For larger fish, 3/0 hooks should be tied on short leaders (three to four inches) to help reduce snags. A single or double hook rig can be used with just enough weight to reach and hold bottom. It is not recommended to have a hook hanging below the sinker, which increases chance for snags. Using a light-poundage leader for sinker attachment (six- or eight-pound test line) allows for the hook(s) to often be saved when sinker becomes fouled. Green crabs are normal bait and, depending on their size, either cut in half or fished whole, if small. In addition, sand crabs, clams, and even gulp crab is often found palatable. But for consistent results, crab is the bait de jour if available. When targeting larger fish (four pounds and up) the best rig for green crabs is a double hook rig where both hooks are inserted in one whole crab. Tog eat the backfin out of crab first. Meaning if a hook is positioned in each section of backfin, chances are increased for hooking up!

"You have another one?" The Fisherman wondered why he asked the obvious question, since Pop's rod was bent over hard. He had four keepers in the box already and his uncle three, while the Fisherman had chalked up a couple shorts.

Watching the two pros set hooks was a thing of beauty. Using sand crabs as bait, on the first tell-tail sign of a bite the hook set was attempted. The Fisherman was amazed how the two toggers honed their skills down to perfection, even after watching them for years hooking tog.

"You two must be able to tell when a tog is getting ready to bite."

It was like psychic powers allowed them to set the hook before the bite. Okay, that may be an exaggeration. But sensing the bite is important. And since the introduction of braided line several years ago, hookup percentages increased significantly over monofilament. In addition, braid performed better when coming into contact with structure and reduced cutoffs. When using large bait (whole green crab or clam) a scant more time is required setting hook. A second tap is generally in order before trying to hookup. In either case, the hook is set with force to penetrate the hard mouth area.

A rod with some backbone helps to drag or pull big tog out of a wreck. Thirty- or forty-pound test line, with drags set to the heavy side, allows the required pressure to be applied. When a fish is hooked, but the line becomes fouled in the structure, giving the fish slack occasionally results in the tog pulling the line free. But more often then not, the fish stays in the structure and a new rig needs to be ready at hand.

Fisherman's father-in-law threw another nice four-pound tog in the box on ice and, with a smile, said, "Hey boy, you gonna help put fish in the box?"

The Fisherman shook his head at his father-in-law. "No, you catch 'em; I'll clean 'em!"

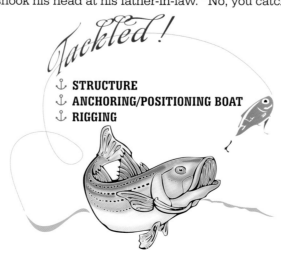

Tackled !

⚓ **STRUCTURE**
⚓ **ANCHORING/POSITIONING BOAT**
⚓ **RIGGING**

When targeting large tog, use two hooks; insert one in each section of backfin. Use sinker and crack top of shell allowing scent to escape.

Fishing wrecks/ structure that receive light fishing pressure often gives up catches like this.

21

22

Chapter 18
Nature's Perfection

The ocean has fascinated the Fisherman ever since childhood—whether searching for live treasures for his aquarium among the inlet jetty rocks on low tide, surf fishing with waves crashing ashore from a stiff northeast breeze, or offshore with his dad fishing upon a long gentle swell out of the south. The ocean was interesting, inspirational, and nurturing to the soul.

Over the years, appreciation and respect for the saltwater environment grew. Sunrises held a special string to the heart. Every day provided a spectacular sight for anyone willing to open eyes and take advantage. It amazed the Fisherman how many charter clients sat in the boat cabin as a new day began, with a miracle occurring on the eastern horizon.

But it was not just sunrises that drew the Fisherman to a life on the water. He appreciated all aspects and learned something new everyday—day after day, studying the weather or why a storm petrel fluttered and appeared to stand on water during tuna chunkin trips, keeping the boat company all day. The petrels reminded the Fisherman of a hummingbird, being able to hover stationary. Being the smallest of sea birds, he often wondered how this tiny fragile-looking bird survived hurricane-force winds offshore, since they only came to shore one time a year to breed.

There are seven different subfamilies of petrels with the Wilson storm petrel common in the mid-Atlantic. Folklore holds that storm petrels are the spirit of sea captains, condemned to fly over the sea for eternity for mistreating crews. Other stories say they are from the souls of sailors who went to their deaths in the depths in the sea. All the Fisherman knew was he enjoyed them and they were a pleasure to have around offshore.

Then there is one of the Fisherman's best friends: the shearwaters. These birds are often used to locate white marlin during the fall bite as fish migrated back south. Keen eyes and height advantage allowed the birds to see balls of baitfish under the surface. The birds swoop back and forth until white marlin forced the bait balls to the surface, where carnage occurred for the baitfish from below and above. There is no mistaking when white marlin are balling bait.

The shearwaters are also a good indication of when schools of tuna are on the move. The birds stay with the school in hope that paths are crossed with baitfish to provide them meals. Yes, there are times when shearwaters are a pain in the rear—like eating chunks of butterfish intended to draw tuna to the transom...or on days when they are intent on snatching trolled ballyhoo bait as their next meal and getting foul hooked.

There are no disappointing sunrises on the ocean; some are just better than others!

Storm petrel in search of breakfast on an ocean that looked like a lake this day.

Going to be a good day of trolling when shearwaters are thick, indicating feeding pelagic. Notice the verticle line in the photo: at the time of this shot the line was rigged with ballyhoo.

Persistence finally paid off for this shearwater who got its meal, along with a trip to the boat. It is impossible at times to keep the birds off bait. Fortunately, the hook did not injure this bird.

Shearwaters are one of the few species of birds that are capable of swimming underwater to obtain a meal—this time butterfish chunks intended for tuna.

The crystal-clear ocean provides an aquarium view of an odd-looking fish: the mola mola.

Water spout.

This Loggerhead turtle was one of the most unusual catches the Fisherman ever witnessed at the end of a line.

But the bird's uniqueness of being able to swim underwater while still being one of the most agile wings on the air is something to marvel.

A charter on one deep drop trip was fortunate to witness a species the Fisherman considered an odyssey of nature. A fish that doesn't really look like a fish and dines on jellyfish. With an average weight in the neighborhood of 1,000 pounds, the mola mola, or more commonly called the ocean sunfish, appears to have no tail. The dorsal fin is often seen at distances and mistaken for a shark fin, until it is observed flopping around on the surface. The mola seldom offers an up-close and personal view before submerging. But this day, while drifting seventy miles off the beach, one swam up to the boat and appeared curious as to what was in its bailiwick—actually turning sideways, looking up to see what was looking back down, right next to the boat. For ten minutes, the fish circled the boat before slowly continuing on its journey to unknown parts.

Of all the things the Fisherman witnessed offshore over the years, water spouts put him in awl several times. Most often, a small front, no more than three or four miles wide with unstable air, could be seen on the radar. Even this small of a storm front can produce waterspouts in the morning. On one occasion, the base of a waterspout was close to a trawler (for size reference) and over 100 yards wide. Being the equivalent of a tornado on land, thoughts were always of the devastation and destruction that would have occurred if what was being witnessed had occurred in a residential neighborhood. Fortunately, the trawler was just out of the path and spared harm. But the "Finger of God" is a beautiful sight to behold.

On one shark charter, a bluefish filet, suspended by a float, began to slowly move on the surface. It was not the typical bite of a shark, let alone a mako, the targeted species. Finally, the hook was set and a heavy weight slowly came towards the boat. It was puzzling what could be on the end of the line, until a loggerhead turtle raised its head with hook clearly visible in corner of mouth.

As the turtle edged closer to the boat, a second loggerhead was observed swimming along side. The first turtle was pulled onto the transom swim platform where it proceeded to hiss and intimidate everyone onboard. The Fisherman began speaking softly, telling the turtle everything would be fine and that the hook needed to be removed. Meanwhile, the other turtle swam back and forth within feet of transom, with head above water watching every move onboard. As pliers were extracted from hip holster, the turtle stopped hissing and raised its head with open mouth, as if in a dentist's office. Being as gentle as possible, while continually speaking softly, the Fisherman extracted the hook as the brown eyes of the turtle looked into his eyes.

Once the hook was removed, the turtle needed no help, but turned and joined its mate to slowly swim away. To this day, the Fisherman seldom tells the story, since those listening roll eyes in disbelief. But that day was as close as the Fisherman ever felt to Nature's perfection.

Chapter 19
Trolling for *Coryphaena hippurus*

Techniques and tips for catching mahi mahi

The name may not sound appealing. However, this fish, baked with lemon and pepper, leaves a clean plate and palate crying for more. The Fisherman could never recall these fish being referred to by their given names for the two varieties: *Coryphaena hippurus* or *Coryphaena equisetic*. But, depending where any angler drops lines, mention mahi mahi, dorado, or dolphin, and everyone lends an ear to catch what's being said. It only takes one encounter with a big bull dolphin (male) with line burning runs and an aerial display that rivals white marlin, to acquire the fever for catching these fish.

Mahi mahi means "strong strong" in Polynesian and is named such for good reason. Pound for pound, they are champions on the end of the line. Blistering runs and aerial displays create shouts of cheer, as does their clean sweet taste at dinner. They are one of the few pelagic currently in no danger of over fishing. With a lifespan of about four or five years, growth is rapid, obtaining a length of forty-five inches within a couple years and the ability to reproduce at eight inches of length. The fishery appears stable and able to support the federal allowance of ten fish per day with no minimal size. Still, anglers should practice catch and release or take only what is necessary for table fare. States such as Georgia and Florida have placed a twenty-inch fork length requirement; hopefully, other states will follow suit to preserve the fishery.

Mahi mahi take up summer residence along the mid-Atlantic when water temperatures climb to around sixty-eight to seventy degrees. Find flotsam or sargassum anywhere offshore and mahi are normally in the vicinity, with decent-sized fish often found within ten miles of the beach. Offshore anglers deciding to suspend trolling to bail mahi, once a school is located under floating debris or a weedline, could be making a mistake (see Chapter 14: Balls of Fun). Doing so removes chances of encountering white marlin, blue marlin, or wahoo that pursue mahi, as well as anglers, for their next meal. Mahi are not the only predator who finds sargassum to their liking! The savvy angler looking for big mahi continues dragging bait in prime waters, the best way to produce true trophy wall hangers.

On several occasions, clients of the Fisherman caught a large bull (male with blunt-looking head) and female (rounded head) simultaneously—confirming that larger fish often swim in pairs and also indicating that when a mahi comes tight on a line, the boat should be kept in gear for multiple hookups.

Flying fish make up about twenty-five percent of a dolphin's diet, supplemented with squid, small fish, and just about anything else that gets too close. The Fisherman prefers skirting ballyhoo in brightly colored skirts or blue hues, but normally, color really didn't seem to be an issue. Many charter captains

The Fisherman's nephew with mahi that would bring a smile
to any angler's face.

This mahi fell for a blue/white Ilander skirted over medium ballyhoo.

actually prefer small, naked ballyhoo. Besides rigged bait, artificial lures, like cedar plugs, zukers, and spoons find success. Trolling speed does not seem to be much of an issue either, if the baits are working/swimming naturally; chances are mahi will find them appetizing, although speeding up can entice lock-jawed fish to the hook. When school-sized mahi are abundant, it is annoying to constantly keep rigging small ballyhoo to catch a couple dozen, and this is when artificial lures really come in handy. In addition, a four- or five-pound dolphin on thirty- or fifty-pound class tackle does not offer much sport. When this happens, drop down to lighter tackle; these same fish become line burners providing fast-action fun.

Anglers heading offshore for a day of trolling normally have forethoughts of doing battle with tuna or marlin. However, when a gaffer (mahi requiring gaff for landing) is hoisted over the transom, cameras are brought out to capture the brilliant colors and angler's smile.

Gaffing Mahi

Here are a few of the Fisherman's tactics when gaffing mahi…

⚓ **When wiring fish,** hold the leader down close to the water to prevent them from jumping and throwing the hook.

⚓ **Dolphin are thin;** do not reach for a big gaff. Use a two-inch or three-inch gaff head on larger fish to simplify gaffing. As seen in the photograph, they twist and turn on a gaff head. The faster the fish can be removed from the water…the better! The Fisherman normally takes a gaff shot at mahi from the top. Being a thin fish it seems to make it easier than trying to come up from the bottom of the fish to gaff.

⚓ **Mahi are not inhalers,** but bite their meal. Keeping bait to the small side increases hook-ups. Missed bites should be dropped back, jerked, and then quickly wound to the boat to entice another strike when trolling.

⚓ **Throwing a wet towel** over the eyes of large fish calms them down before beating the boat to pieces.

⚓ **To prevent fish spraying blood** everywhere and bruising ankles, throw them directly into the killbox and close the lid. Grab an extra rod; while the fish is in the box, it normally dislodges the hook within a short time. When finished with the smiles for the camera, ice down well to preserve the meat's fresh flavor and texture or release to provide action another day.

Fisherman gaffs a nice mahi. Using a small three-inch gaff head works better on the thin-body mahi compared to a large gaff head.

These fish are the ideal pelagic to cause cockpit chaos. After the first one is hooked, maintain boat speed and leave all bait in the water. This often equates into most, if not all, the rods going down. When trolling a weed line, tighten up the spread to prevent long lines from fouling in grass, and keep a sharp eye on the spread. There is no better place to see the food chain in action than a weed line. Predators, like white and blue marlin, prey upon small mahi. So keep a keen eye; use polarized glasses to enhance vision to make suspended fish easier to observe.

Mahi are extremely colorful and reflect a wide range of brilliant colors. In order to capture all their beauty on camera, do so when the fish is first brought onboard. Coloration quickly fades to plain, white/silvery once out of the water for any period of time.

Mahi of this size are a trophy in any angler's fishing tale.

Tackled!

⚓ **LOCATING**
⚓ **BAIT**
⚓ **GAFFING**

Chapter 20
Nine No No's

Mistakes no angler wants to make!

"NO! NO! GET THE ROD OFF THE GUNWALE!"
The bluefin was punishing the angler. It was hooked up while chunkin within the fleet and the Fisherman's attention had been on maneuvering the boat away from others. When he turned around, the tired angler was just about to do the unthinkable. The rod had just been purchased on the boat's charge account a couple weeks earlier after another client broke a rod by laying it on the gunwale when a big bluefin sapped the angler's strength. The boat owner was not very happy about the charge. The Fisherman in no way wanted to give the owner more bad news. And now another angler was about to do the same thing. The Fisherman felt bad for yelling and startling the angler, but it was over and done with; the rod was still intact!

Charter boat fishing gives the Fisherman a front row seat, observing anglers committing mistakes daily. Often, he felt like Bill Murray in the movie *Groundhog Day*, only with the script changed to a boat at sea watching fishermen make the same mistakes over and over, day after day. The majority of these anglers have little offshore fishing experience. However, even veterans made errors from time to time when embattled with a tuna that often outweighed them. Now and then, Lady Luck jumped onboard before the boat pulled out of the slip and fish were boated despite errors. But more often than not, these mistakes cost the angler his/her fish, and often the fish of a lifetime. Testing one's fishing savvy against large pelagic demands flawless performance out of equipment and effort from the angler, if success is to be achieved.

Bluefin, yellowfin, marlin, or any other pelagic has the ability to put a world of hurt on an angler. This is evident by the look of fatigue the Fisherman observed worn on faces in contest with these tough competitors.

Following is a list of what the Fisherman calls "nine no no's." If paid attention to, there is a possibility that less four-letter words might be uttered, not to mention reducing the opportunity of line separation.

❶ Placing a thumb on the spool to add a "little" extra drag in order to stop a fish from spooling the reel is like trying to stop a freight train.
The first runoff is normally the longest. Trust must be placed in the reel's drag system. Drags are preset at twenty-five to thirty percent of the line's breaking strength and there is very little room for more pressure when a fish is screaming south from a northbound transom. It is difficult watching line disappear from the spool and thoughts of trying to slow down a fish by adding just a little more pressure is only natural. However, this action has disaster written all over it. Turn the boat and chase, if necessary.

❷ Trying to retrieve line against the drag is a waste of energy. This is the one time an angler actually has the opportunity to rest; take advantage of it. Hold the rod at a forty-five-degree angle during runoffs; begin reeling and working the fish once it stops taking line.

❸ There is no need for the "hit the captain on the bridge" move. The Fisherman is not sure what anglers try to accomplish by lifting the rod high over their heads and leaning back as far as possible. Don't do it! This move creates friction and increases line tension that pushes a line near, if not past, its breaking point (not to mention the move tics off the captain!). Fish are worked by raising the rod to the one o'clock position, then retrieve line while lowering the rod to near three o'clock position. Always begin winding "BEFORE" lowering the rod tip to prevent slack in the line.

❹ Once a hook is set, it cannot be improved upon. Jerking and pulling on the rod to "set the hook better" will only tear at the hole where the hook has penetrated through the mouth. An exception to this rule is when billfishing. Marlin and sailfish have hard bony mouths that are difficult to penetrate. If J-hook is being used, several short, firm jerks often is better than one hard set. If using circle hooks for billfish, allow the fish to hook itself. Just wind when the line comes tight. A circle hook cannot be set. Circle hooks are gaining popularity with billfish enthusiasts; the hookup percentage is better than J-hooks. If you are not using them, now is the time to consider doing so.

❺ Don't be impatient! Battling a large pelagic on a 30 or even 50 class outfit is going to take some time. It takes constant pressure and remaining calm to land fish at a five to one, or better, line ratio.

❻ Rest is not an option. Holding the rod with a fish at the other end of the line will not put the fish in the boat. Angler rest = fish rest! Rest only when the fish is stripping line, otherwise, lift the rod smoothly and retrieve line with the reel. Arms cannot hold a rod under constant pressure for very long. A harness is imperative in keeping the heat turned up on a fish. By transferring pressure off the arms to the back, odds of success shifts to the angler.

❼ As mentioned in the beginning of the chapter, never rest a rod on the gunwale. Bluefin are notorious for getting directly under the boat. This means standup fishing to prevent line from coming in contact with the chine of the boat. Stand up whenever a fish sounds under the boat, unless you like the sound of line separation. It is hard to imagine that a person's body can be punished more than in this situation. First, the lower back feels as if it is about to explode. Next, a hand is placed on the gunwale to relieve back pressure. Then, ever so slowly, the rod dips down towards the gunwale. The rod cannot rest on the gunwale! Rods are constructed to spread pressure out over the length of the rod. When placed on a gunwale, all pressure becomes bottled up in front half of the rod ending in a broken rod. Anglers yelled at to get the rod off the gunwale normally draws a look of "what the hell am I supposed to do?" One option is to hand the rod off.

The other option is to hit the gym during the winter. At the very least, keep the back straight to reduce lower spine stress. Just keep the rod off the gunwale. Placing a rod on the gunwale under pressure is a sure way to buy a new expensive rod.

❽ Never assume the fight is over. After a two-, three-, or four-hour tug of war, anglers tend to let their guard down when the leader is finally in hand and the fish is being wired. Anglers need to stay focused. Back off the drag slightly and be alert in case the fish cannot be held and leader needs to be released. Yes, even after a couple hours, fish still can have energy. Collapse only after the fish is in on the deck!

❾ And finally the number-one reason fish are lost on the Fisherman's charters: the angler stops winding. Fish that turn and charge the boat may create the illusion that the hook has been thrown. Now is the time for the following three steps: point the rod toward the fish; wind fast as possible; prepare for the line to become taut again. Standing with a look of disappointment without a good grip on the rod, whining "he got away" spells disaster. The Fisherman unfortunately has seen a couple outfits glistening and flashing as they headed towards the bottom in 100 fathoms of water!

Chapter 21

Wahoo

A sudden change is noticed when walking out the door one morning. The air has a different feel of crispness; the sweet fragrances of summer have gone overnight and have been replaced by a cool, clean aroma that makes a person feel good to be alive. Fall arrived! And, with it, offshore fishing takes on a new twist. Migrating fish moving south after spending summer off the northeast coastline offers fishing opportunity not available during the days of summer. White marlin certainly gets the most attention this time of year while balling bait. This bite often creates double-digit releases that headlines most offshore news. Longfin tuna also adds a new twist out on the edge. Inshore, striped bass is all the rage. And, in-between these bite locations, lays the twenty- and thirty-fathom lumps where one of the fastest swimming fish in the ocean (not to mention one of the *best* on a plate) arrives to fill stomachs during migration: the wahoo. Wahoo are caught all summer long, but fall is when there is what might be called an actual wahoo bite.

The Fisherman concentrates on wahoo a few trips each year. The trolling spread is set just for these speedsters, who are able to obtain speeds close to sixty MPH in short bursts, putting tackle to the extreme test. Occasionally, other species find the trolled bait appetizing, but wahoo is the targeted species that provides the fishing fun.

The perfect fall offshore weather forecast was all it took for a buddy of the Fisherman to call with the question, "Want to run offshore with the kids? They want to go fishing."

The Fisherman thought...kids want to go fishing—yeah, right, the kids! His buddy's three children did love to fish and were excellent anglers. The Fisherman always enjoyed spending days on the ocean in their company. But the Fisherman knew it was a ploy. The wife would be fine with her husband taking the kids fishing. But, if the husband had wanted to go alone, well, then there might be a problem!

"Sure, a few wahoo were caught last week on the inner lumps; want to give them a shot?"

Details were worked out and, a couple days later, the Fisherman, his buddy, the two sons, and daughter were running on a flat sea heading to an area known as the Sausages. The bottom consisted of several lumps, beginning on the twenty-fathom line, fanning out to thirty fathoms. Full of bottom character, all the edges created uprisings, rips, and swirling water, which produced prime fishing for all species—but none more so than wahoo. Wahoo, while not a school fish, can be found traveling in packs during the fall migration. Find one and normally there are more feeding in the general area.

Another beautiful sunrise brings with it the promise of a great day offshore.

Puffer fish found in patch of grass. At end of day, when cleaning fish, stomachs were full of what apparently were… little tasty treats!

Mouth of wahoo needs to be treated with respect. Fisherman had a wahoo slice his leg open one day as the fish came over the gunnel when he was not paying attention.

The Fisherman's son and lifelong buddy are all smiles displaying a double header; both wahoo were caught off a double rigged planer.

The boat slowed and spread was set. When wahoo fishing, the Fisherman always deployed a double planner rig for deep baits. This rig utilized a Z-wing (or any large planner); it is attached to the boat transom by eighty feet of 150-pound test Dacron. This places the planner at a depth close to fifty feet. Two baits were run off this rig. First, a rigged medium/large ballyhoo, skirted in red/black or black/purple, was placed 150 feet behind transom. A rubber band was then twisted around the fishing line several times before a double end snap swivel was attached to the rubber band and then snapped to the planer line. As line slowly spools off reel, the snap slides down the line until reaching the Z-wing. Rod is placed in holder and drag set with lure being trolled at a depth of approximately 50 feet. When wahoo strikes the rubber band breaks and game on. A second line is set the same way as the first, with the exception that the bait is set 100 feet behind the boat and only twenty-five feet of line is spooled off the reel, placing bait at that depth.

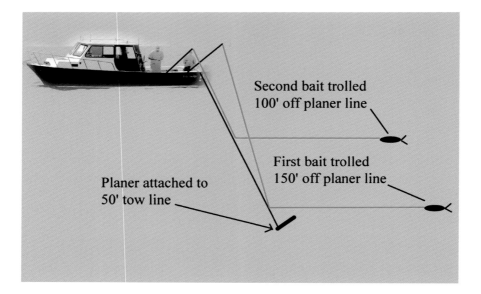

Second bait trolled 100' off planer line

First bait trolled 150' off planer line

Planer attached to 50' tow line

The remaining rods are rigged with ballyhoo skirted in dark colors. All leaders must be wire; monofilament does not stand a chance in the wahoo's mouth of razor-sharp teeth.

After thirty minutes of fruitless trolling, the Fisherman was somewhat disgusted. "Water is green; lets pick up and run." And with that statement lines were cranked in and, within minutes, the boat was up on plane heading east. After covering a few miles, a two-degree temperature break was found and water changed from green to a decent bluish/green.

There were patches of weeds all along the temperature break with just enough small mahi underneath to keep the kids busy on the rods. Then, during one lull, the kids took notice of something in a batch of weeds. They dug a net out of the cabin and started dipping at grass as the boat trolled by.

The Fisherman always thought everyday was a learning experience and this day was no different. It was another first as small Puffer fish were hiding in, or swimming near, every small patch of weeds. This prompted the kids to do what they do best: have fun! Occasionally, a mahi would come over the transom, but as soon as the line was reset, the kids were back at scooping up clumps of weeds with Puffer fish. Their five-gallon bucket aquarium also contained tiny lobsters and varieties of other small sea creatures that had taken refuge in the weeds. The kids were not the only people onboard intrigued!

But, the net was quickly thrown down when the planer rod's reel screamed. A wahoo had found the black/purple Ilander skirted over horse ballyhoo to his liking. The daughter was up next and, for the following thirty minutes, played a game of tug and war, until besting her opponent and the gaff was sunk.

Several more mahi were boated and one more wahoo managed to miss the hook after cutting a horse ballyhoo in half but, unfortunately, did not come back to finish the meal. Wahoo use this technique when feeding: cut prey in half and quickly circle back around to finish the meal—meaning, if a Wahoo bite does not come tight, free-spool as if billfishing. This sometimes results in a hookup. With school the next day for our anglers, we called it a day at 2:30 with a forty-five-mile-run back to the inlet. While cleaning fish, every stomach was full of Puffer fish, and to think we left our Puffer fish rigs at home!

Next day, after posting the fishing update on his blog, the Fisherman got a call from one of his sons and another buddy. Both inquired when they were going wahoo fishing! Two days later, the boat broke the inlet at sunrise, once again heading to the Sausages with wahoo the target. The wind had swung from east to south and, with it, produced one of those rare, warm falls days. Luckily, before the wind shifted from the east, it blew the bluish/green water west into the twenty-fathom line. The Sausages produced mahi, along with several wahoo this day, including a double header—both came off the Z-wing. It was a couple days of what could be called, fast-fall fishing!

Tackled!

⚓ **DOUBLE RIGGED PLANER**
⚓ **COLOR SENSITIVE**

Chapter 22

Can I Die?

Understanding seasickness

First, a nauseous feeling swells over the body. Then moisture begins to gather in the mouth, followed by an eruption down in the pit of the stomach. A moment later, a perfectly good breakfast is wasted over the transom, along with the thought, "has anyone died from being seasick?" Well, no one has died to the Fisherman's knowledge, although he has watched hundreds of anglers wish they *were* dead! Being sick makes for a real long day offshore.

What Causes Seasickness?

The inner ear controls our balance. Seasickness, or motion sickness, occurs when the inner ear tells the brain that the body is moving, caused by boat movement, waves, etc. However, the eyes are fixed and stable, telling the brain that the body is *not* moving. The brain reacts in confusion causing seasickness symptoms. Maybe a better example: You are at one of those great IMAX theatres watching a 3-D movie; your eyes send signals to the brain that the body is moving, but your inner ear says, "Nope, sitting still." The brain becomes confused and the body responds with feelings of motion sickness for some people.

Navy research has shown that about one percent of the population does not get motion sickness. Ten percent rarely have a problem, leaving the rest a chance of getting sick anytime they board a boat. Navy studies have also shown that over-the-counter remedies, such as Dramamine, are moderately effective for most people, with prescription medications being the most effective. In controlled real-motion trials with natural remedies, such as ginger or pressure-point therapy, anxiety was reduced; but, overall, these remedies were found to be ineffective. The good news: the Navy found that prescribing Scopolamine as a nasal spray was highly effective for preventing seasickness. Research should be completed within the next year, so help may be on the way for anglers who suffer with nauseous feelings.

Recommendations to Avoid Seasickness

- ⚓ **Don't try to drink** all the alcohol in town the night before running offshore.
- ⚓ **Follow directions** when taking over-the-counter medications.
- ⚓ **Stay away from the** "all you can eat" breakfast buffet.
- ⚓ **If feeling nauseous,** stay out of the cabin and focus on the horizon.
- ⚓ **Finally, if you get deathly sick,** waste breakfast over the gunwale, not in the head where it has to be cleaned up!

Husband is consoled by wife at start of what was to be a very *loooong* day of trolling for him.

Chapter 23
X Chromosome

Females and fishing

One out of five saltwater anglers with rod in hand have the X chromosome running through their bodies. This equates to about 7.5 million women. And these women control the purse strings of the 31-billion-dollar-a-year recreational, saltwater fishing industry. And if you don't believe women control the purse strings, then apparently you have never paid attention to the interior of a serious sportsfishing boat... Or checked out the female angler clothing sections at Cabela's or Bass Pro Shops... Nor happened to be in the sporting goods store and observed the Fisherman explaining (begging?) to his wife why "they" need another Shimano Trinidad 6.2 to 1 high speed reel for deep dropping.

The Fisherman's recreational fishing time is normally spent with his wife. And don't let his daughters, daughter-in-laws, or sister-in-laws see rods being rigged the night before a trip! Why? Because technology has made the days of bulky 50 and 80 class outfits all but obsolete, if one desires, when offshore. Lightweight, easy-to-handle outfits allow women (and men) to beat up on most pelagic whether trolling, jigging, or casting.

Although the Fisherman never kept records on this fact, probably fifty percent of charters included women. Fishing is a unisex sport and, if you want to keep your fishing partner smiling while including her on offshore adventures, here are a few points that Y chromosome people might want to keep in mind...

⚓ **Bathroom:** Provide some type of head and don't forget tissue paper.

⚓ **Fashion Statement:** Women like to be dressed for the part—even sixty-five miles offshore. Go shopping with her and pick out a fishing outfit.

⚓ **Keep it Simple:** Everything can't be taught in one day. Begin with, "This is how to hold the rod and wind the reel." Everything else will be learned over time.

⚓ **Weather:** Don't press it; no one enjoys a day offshore when the weather is rough.

⚓ **Patience:** You are sharing the joy of fishing and spending quality time together. Tangles, lost fish, mistakes, baiting hooks, and questions should be taken in stride (well, maybe not lost fish!)

And most importantly: when your better-half out fishes you...ACT HAPPY!

Female angler population is growing offshore. Are you ready?

Chapter 24

Burn a Hole!

Charter boat trolling technique

Fishing reports are often read in disbelief—ten, fifteen, even twenty yellowfin or white marlin reportedly caught by some boats. The information leaves many anglers with one question. How? The answer: the most was made of each bite opportunity. Charter boats (and serious offshore anglers) are not satisfied with a single hookup. Two, three, or four rods down at a time fills killboxes and put smiles on clients' faces. The following technique is used to catch multiple tuna and works for other species, as well. Multiple hookups occasionally occur by chance, but to occur routinely, the bite must be created.

Often, after the first fish is screaming drag, the boat is slowed as someone yells to clear rods. Hold on a minute, clear rods? If rods are cleared, all chances of catching additional fish are lost. If you're content with catching one fish at a time (all anglers were at one time) then clear lines. However, if you want to make the most out of every bite opportunity, the boat needs to maintain speed and make a turn to the side where the fish is running. The wideness or sharpness of this turn depends on the fish. The maneuver tries to circle the fish. Constant pressure must be kept on the fish by keeping a bend in the rod. At times, this may require winding very quickly to keep slack line from occurring. Also, pay attention to the bow in the line and try to keep it at a minimum. The crew should have grabbed the remaining rods and added extra movement to bait, enticing additional bites.

When the Fisherman has a charter with inexperienced clients, instead of having everyone jerk lines on a bite, speeding up often induces additional bites. As the boat continues to troll, just make sure the first fish is not run over. Of course, the amount of line stripped by the first fish dictates how long trolling can continue. Burning a hole, as it is called, accounts for those stories of every rod going down with a half-dozen tuna caught at a time or triple header white marlin hook-ups.

The Fisherman headed south and fished out of Los Suenos, Costa Rica, during a couple off seasons in the Northeast. Known for its outstanding sailfishing and catches of twenty or more sails a day, there is no better place to exemplify burning a hole. The sails are not caught one fish at a time (well, technically), but two or three at a time. The shown photograph of the plotter screen is typical at day's end. The eleven circles on the screen represent eleven bites, which accounted for two blue marlin and twenty-three sailfish this day. Burning a hole in the ocean is a proven technique that works and creates multiple hookups.

Multiple hook-ups cause havoc in the pit, so it is to the crew's advantage for everyone to be well-versed and capable of performing every task in the pit when

The Fisherman's son gives thumbs-up after crew went four-for-four on yellowfin, while burning a hole in the ocean.

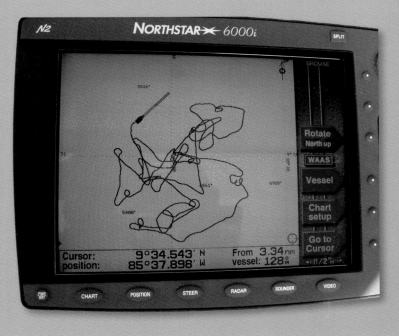

The eleven circles on the screen represent eleven bites, which accounted for two blue marlin and twenty-three sailfish this day, while using the "burn a hole" technique.

the bite occurs. Going over a plan of action on the ride out to the canyons is well worth the time to prepare for later when opportunity knocks. Everyone needs to know their assigned jobs when the captain shouts to clear lines, which means winding teasers in, pulling dredges, and wiring fish for gaff or release without turning the pit into a cluster where fish are lost.

As the saying goes, "It is better to be lucky than good." Maybe, but being at the right location when the bite turns on occurs by either pure luck or careful planning. Spend time around a marina and you'll observe the same charter boats coming to the dock day after day with fish. Their success, as simple or stupid as it sounds, is by concentrating efforts where fish are located, not by sheer luck.

Good Water

Conversations surrounding good bites often refer to "good" water. Anglers consider good water as clean, clear, and blue. Pelagic also consider these conditions good, assuming water temperature is to their liking. However, the number one contributing factor in finding your quarry is the presence of food. Without a food source, fish are practically non-existent. The best bite occurs when bait is abundant in a given location, which draws fish to feed. Fish stay in an area as long as baitfish and the right conditions are present. Locating a promising location is like constructing a puzzle: when all the pieces fit, everything comes together, creating opportunity, which in turn leads to success. However, there is a problem when fishing clean, clear, water: it does not contain plankton, which begins the food chain. This means, if all time is spent trolling crystal clear, clean, water, chances of finding a great bite are slim at best. No plankton = few fish.

Plankton is found in green/dirty water or when deep nutrient-rich water rises in an upwelling, warms, and blooms into phytoplankton.

In simplistic terms, fishing an edge between green and blue water is one of the best areas to concentrate efforts, since the food chain is present. Short transition distance in water clarity between dirty and clean normally results in better fishing. This is often where temperature breaks are found as well. A two-degree break is all that's necessary. Along the Atlantic seaboard, temperature breaks are found when warm, clean, Gulf Stream water pushes in from the east and meets green inshore water containing plankton. This can be just a finger of water jutting off or an eddy of water that broke off the Gulf Stream and drifted east. Find blue water forming a wall against green water, throw in a temperature break and, in all probability, baitfish can be found somewhere along the line with pelagic in pursuit.

Obtaining Information

With the price of fuel, covering a lot of ocean territory in search of fish is not the best plan of action for an angler's pocketbook. Since ninety-nine percent of anglers are not fortunate enough to fish everyday to track good water, other options are required for deciding where to fish. There is no better information source than making friends with a couple charter captains or mates at your local marina, who are in the deep everyday with clients. Of course, they may have tight lips when keeping a good bite under wraps and only reveal information after the fact.

Joining a fishing club or becoming active on fishing websites, like www.Sportfishermen.com or www.tidalfish.com, are great places to make acquaintances and exchange recent fishing information. Many tackle shops and marinas have websites with daily-catch information.

But for most anglers, it comes down to making an educated guess based on fragmented or sketchy information. A subscription to one of the satellite sea-surface temperature (SST) websites is invaluable for locating temperature breaks and warm eddies of water. In addition to paid sites, free services, such as those provided by Rutgers University's Coastal Ocean Observation Lab, provide current temperature information (www.marine.rutgers.edu).

Some services even show baitfish concentrations. While satellites do not pick up actual pods of baitfish, weedlines, etc., they do identify plankton in the form of Chlorophyll, which is ideal for baitfish presence. If checking Chlorophyll overlays, high levels indicate nutrient-rich water, while lower levels indicate clean, blue water. Locate areas where these two clash, throw in a temperature break and, once again, you've found the numbers to punch in the GPS to begin a day offshore. These edges often contain flotsam or weed lines, which enhance fishing conditions. Of course, nothing surpasses an angler's actual knowledge obtained once on site. Water temperature, color, and sea-life conditions needs to be assessed to determine which edges to concentrate trolling efforts. Working edges where these conditions exist normally result in an ocean brimming with activity and certainly increases the chances of burning a hole in the ocean with bent rods!

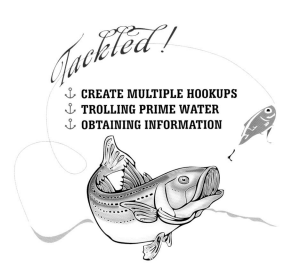

Tackled!

⚓ **CREATE MULTIPLE HOOKUPS**
⚓ **TROLLING PRIME WATER**
⚓ **OBTAINING INFORMATION**

Chapter 25

Bluefin Strategies

Understanding bluefin behavior to increase hookups

"SOMEONE ELSE TAKE THE ROD; I CAN'T DO IT!"
The words had been uttered in the pit many times before and, once again, an angler's anguish caused the phrase to be blurted out as he was beaten into submission. Pound for pound, no other member of the tuna family covers more foreheads in beads of sweat than bluefin. *Thunnus thynnus*, the big dog, called so not only because it is the biggest member of the tuna family, but also, in the Fisherman's opinion and that of many other anglers, due to having the ability to punish anglers like no other tuna. If your idea of a phenomenal fishing day is to climb off the boat feeling like you've been stuck in the ring for fifteen rounds with the champ getting the $%#@ beat out of you, then bluefin just might be your preferred targeted species.

Bluefin are unique in the liquid environment. Unlike other members of the tuna family, they are capable of adjusting body temperature to the surrounding water. This gives them the ability to feed throughout the water column, especially near the bottom on inshore shoals. The Tuna Research and Conservation Center, in cooperation with universities, did an extensive survey tracking bluefin with satellite technology. The findings, although not targeted for recreational anglers, nonetheless can make better bluefin anglers by using the research.

In the study, fish were caught off the North Carolina coast. Pop-off satellite tags were placed on the fish before being released. The tags stayed on the fish anywhere from sixty to ninety days, after which they release and float to the surface. The information stored in the tags then transmits to the ARGO satellite system. The collected information is not only interesting, but gives anglers a better understanding of how tuna behave within their environment, which can be used when targeting the species.

Bluefin tuna travel remarkable distances. The farthest distance covered in ninety days was 1,670 nautical miles. One bluefin traveled 1,242 nautical miles in sixty days. Bluefin are capable of traveling, on average, three-quarters of a mile every hour. It stands to reason that individual fish may not remain in a given location for an extended period of time.

Temperature preference data indicates that tuna have extraordinary tolerances for temperature swings. They were found to spend time in water ranging from 42.8 to 75.2 degrees. One of the tuna's daily average for sixty days was 51.8. How can they do this? Even with staying in this cooler water, bluefin are able to maintain a body temperature of seventy-seven to eighty degrees. This ability to conserve metabolic heat allows them to be caught in waters that anglers normally may not place bait—specifically, below the thermalcline or near the bottom.

Bluefin tuna like this certainly test an angler's ability.

Available food is probably a better indicator of where bluefin can be found than water temperature. When sonar is not indicating any baitfish in water column, but sand eels are showing up on the bottom, chances are pretty good that this is where the bluefin will be found.

Another satellite tagging study showed that bluefin spend forty percent of their time in the top thirty-foot layer of water during summer, when water temperatures are the warmest. During the winter, when there are mixed layers of water, the vertical distribution of tuna expanded towards deeper water. Conclusion: bluefin tuna do not spend the majority of their time above the thermalcline anytime during the year. In addition, the fish showed distinctive vertical movement during periods of dawn and dusk. It should come as interest that once dawn breaks, tuna make a very slow and steady descent from near the surface, to a depth of eighty-two feet. Remarkably, it took the fish forty minutes to achieve this depth movement. Just the opposite was observed at dusk, when the fish took approximately forty minutes to rise near the surface. This information should give an idea as to where to place baits.

⚓ **Early morning and evening,** fish near the surface.
⚓ **Midday,** bait placement should be deeper in the water column.

Studies such as these provide knowledge to develop fishing strategies.

There are two ways of catching bluefin: trolling or chunkin. To apply information from the study, this chapter will concentrate on trolling strategies (for chunkin information see Chapter 13: Bluefin).

Trolling patterns need to vary, depending on the size of bluefin available at any given time. Smaller bluefin often find feeding at the transom to their liking on Cedar plugs, Zukers, and rig baits pulled in a tight pattern. Medium bluefin (80-150 pounds), on the other hand, are not as apt to take flat lines. Short and long riggers produce most of the fish. Also, way way back lines are extremely productive. Way way back means trolling bait 200 or more yards behind the transom. A large, naked ballyhoo or horse ballyhoo skirted in a Crystal or blue/white Ilander is hard to beat in this position.

The Fisherman normally pulls three way back lines. Two are off long riggers and baits are set at 600 feet and 800 feet. The third line is pulled off a planer with bait set 500 feet behind transom at a depth of approximately fifty feet, which is normally just below the thermocline. This bait is a large ballyhoo skirted in a purple/black Ilander or pink skirt. It is imperative to check these baits often, as they seem to pick up everything floating in the ocean. One way to ease the chore of winding in long lines is to use a battery-operated drill with connection that fits over the reel handle. This connection piece can be purchased for most popular reels or, if blessed with a little mechanical skill, can be constructed out of a piece of one-inch starboard and one-quarter-inch bolt. It is a two-person operation to retrieve lines: one to assure line is taken in without line buildup, the other to operate the drill.

On any given day, it is impossible to say how fish are going to feed behind the boat. But until daily feeding habits are known, it is a wise choice to start with what normally produces.

Spreader bars work off short riggers, period. Success can be achieved with many different-colored bars and, on some days, color makes no difference. The multi or psycho color's popularity has been near the top of the list the last few years, with green and pink also popular. Of course, spreader bars are not the only ticket to bluefin. The blue/white Ilander skirted over a ballyhoo, mentioned earlier, is first choice bait and hard to beat when trolled in any position. In the early morning and on overcast days, a black/purple Ilander skirted over ballyhoo works well. There are anglers who

A cordless drill not only saves an angler's arms from winding in way way back lines, but it also saves valuable fishing time by allowing bait to remain in water longer.

A blue/white Ilander skirted over a horse ballyhoo trolled way way back accounted for this 150-pound bluefin.

swear by ballyhoo skirted in pink. Then there are days when no color seems to attract attention and naked horse ballyhoo puts fish on the end of the line.

The bluefin study indicated that fish spend the majority of time deep in the water column. This does not mean they are feeding. However, it only makes sense to place bait in this vicinity to try and entice bites, especially during the middle of the day. A planer rig is often the ticket to a successful day of bluefin fishing. There are a few options for utilizing and rigging a planer.

The easiest way is to run the planer on a static line attached to the boat. A release device is rigged to the end of the planer or placed in the static line five feet above the planner for fishing line attachment. Place bait 300-500 feet behind the boat before inserting fishing line in planer release clip. Another option is to use a double snap swivel with a rubber band (as mentioned in Chapter 21: Wahoo). To use this technique, again place the bait 300-500 feet behind the boat. Now wrap the #64 rubber band around the fishing line several times. The two ends of the rubber band are then attached to one end of the double snap swivel. The other end of the double snap swivel is clipped onto the planer line. As the fishing line is slowly let out, the swivel slides down to the planer, locating the bait at whatever depth the planer is set. Place rod in the holder and set the drag. When bluefin strikes, the rubber band breaks, allowing the fish to be fought. It is recommended to remove planer from water after hookup to eliminate possibility of fish becoming entangled and to also allow the boat to back down if necessary.

Z-Wing is the Fisherman's first choice, but all these planers get bait down.

- ⚓ **Sea Striker,** Size #8, $20
- ⚓ **Old Salty,** Size #32, $25
- ⚓ **Z-Wing,** $50

If the boat is equipped with downrigger, a ball weight causes too much drag and must be replaced with a planer. Before using, check with the downrigger manufacturer to make sure the pressure exerted by a planer will not bend/snap the downrigger arm. Also, cable hums when trolled at 6 or 7 knots and needs to be replaced with one of the new braided lines.

The deep bait often receives the most attention from bluefin. Besides the black/purple or pink skirt rigged over large or horse ballyhoo on the planer rig, do not discount a lure that has been around for years: a 3½ Drone spoon in silver or white. It can be counted on to take its fair share of bluefin as well.

Ice, ice, and more ice needs to be onboard. To maintain quality of flavor, the bluefin flesh needs to cool down quickly. The image showing the tournament fish is being unloaded to be weighted. An insulated bag was used, even after being in the bag all day, ice can still be observed. These bags are an angler's blessing when it comes to a boat not having a killbox large enough for the catch. If this bluefin were not a tournament fish, it would have been dressed (gutted) and stomach packed in ice to preserved the flavor. Don't allow a quality catch to be ruined by not having ice onboard.

Tackled!

- ⚓ PREFERRED WATER
- ⚓ DEPTH
- ⚓ WAY BACK TROLLING RIGS
- ⚓ PLANER STRATEGY

Chapter 26
Three Fingers

Old fisherman trick to increase catches

It was spring of 1973. The small combination drug store/restaurant was hidden away in a little town on the lower Eastern Shore of Virginia, on the ocean side of the peninsula. Walking through the front door was like stepping back in time. The man behind the cash register spoke in a southern draw with his "Howdy." The greeting was accompanied by a friendly smile. Behind him, on the wall, were old black-and-white photos of big black drum, large bluefin, and even white marlin hanging from an old beam on a wharf. The anglers, some smiling, some serious, were holding split bamboo rods in many photos.

"Just sit anywhere, menus are on the tables."

Underfoot, the old, wooden floor creaked when walked upon. The room had a feel of nostalgia and charm. Apparently, this was the place to eat from the look of the full tables, with people mostly appearing to be anglers, sitting with metal trays as if in an Army mess hall. The room's aroma danced in the nostrils from trays piled high with delicious-looking entrees. An angler at the boat ramp had suggested the place while the Fisherman was pulling the boat, after a long day of not catching any black drum. It appeared the angler knew what he was talking about when it came to eating dinner. The Fisherman thought maybe he should have asked the man how to catch drum.

This was the Fisherman's first black drum trip. A couple friends chartered a boat the week before out of Crisfield, Virginia, and caught several black drum up to sixty pounds—even had photos to prove it. The following week, the Fisherman was heading south on Route 113 in his old van, dragging a nineteen-footer down to the lower part of the Virginia peninsula for a few days to tangle with the bottom-feeding beasts. A couple of his regular fishing buddies joined him. Everyone was excited; after all, how hard could it be to catch a drum?

On this first day of fishing, the Fisherman found the fleet anchored up near buoy C-10. Finding space within the fleet of 100 or so boats, the anchor was sent towards bottom. Drum were observed caught from time to time, but no bent rods occurred on the Fisherman's boat. Now, at day's end, the crew was looking for an open table to plant their tired bottoms and fill their stomachs. Conversation during their delicious dinner of veal cutlets was mostly whining about not catching fish that day—and trying to figure out what should be changed for the next day.

As plates were just about to be licked clean, from the next table came, "Ya should be out there naw."

The Fisherman glanced up and said, "Excuse Me?"

The old timer had a graying beard and a dark-skinned face, with deep-edged lines from years of being on the water or in fields plowing under a blistering sun. His bibbed overhauls had seen better days, as did the tattered long-sleeve flannel shirt. He was alone and apparently had been listening to the conversation.

The old timer studied the Fisherman up and down a couple seconds before continuing in his lower Eastern Shore dialect, "Ya sittin' here and ole drum are chompin' right naw."

The Fisherman was never shy about asking questions concerning how to catch fish and, for the next half hour, after sliding his chair over to the table, the old timer shared years of experience, explaining how to catch black drum. The information consisted of tides, anchoring on hard-bottom edges, chumming sea clams, rigging, and the most important advice: during evenings, fish when the sun is three fingers off the water.

When the conversation came to an end, the Fisherman thanked him and offered to buy dinner, but the old timer declined as he picked up his check and walked towards the register. After paying his bill, the old timer turned and, before walking out the door, shouted over, "Good luck."

It was a brief encounter and the only time the Fisherman saw the man, but he was thankful for the chance meeting and, today, he is still using the old timer's advice—forty years later.

Next day, the Fisherman's boat was anchored on an edge where hard-shell bottom dropped off from fifteen feet down to thirty feet of water. When current started moving on the incoming tide and six hours later on the outgoing, a bite developed on both and black drum were caught.

But the real action came as the sun set. With an outstretched arm, three fingers were placed on the horizon several times waiting for the sun to touch the top finger, just as the old timer had demonstrated sitting at the table. It seemed to take forever, but finally the sun rested upon the three fingers. Low and behold, a rod bent over, followed by another; all four rods came tight, giving the anglers more than they could have hoped for. Looking up, the Fisherman noticed most of the boats had called it a day, but the few remaining boats all seemed to be hooked up as well.

It was the end to a fantastic day of black drum fishing and the beginning of many more days just like it, thanks to an old timer who took a novice under his wing and shared his knowledge and experience.

Since that day, seldom have three fingers failed catching black drum in the evening. But more importantly, over the years, three fingers has worked time and again offshore. As the sun sets in the western sky, a bite normally develops each evening, just the opposite of the bite that develops at first light each day. Three fingers has worked for catching bluefin, yellowfin, and bailing mahi.

The Fisherman (far left, when he still had hair!) and buddies smile with black drum from first successful day using "Three Fingers" technique.

Having a bad day of fishing? If you find yourself offshore late in the day, still waiting on fish in the killbox, and don't mind running to port in the dark, it just might be worth the effort to stick it out for a little longer and give three fingers a shot!

Chapter 27
Fun in the Sun

Fishing the barrier island of Assateague and Chincoteague

The Fisherman is blessed to live on the eastern shore of Maryland. Between the Chesapeake Bay and Atlantic Ocean, it is an angler's paradise—not to mention the crabbing, clamming, swimming, and numerous other outdoor activities that can be found. And there is no better place to find this type of activity than on a thin sliver of sand known as Assateague Island. If you're looking for a vacation where an outdoor family can really enjoy themselves, consider the Eastern Shore of Maryland.

The island begins at the Ocean City, Maryland, inlet and runs south to the inlet at Chincoteague, Virginia. Three agencies are charged with protection of this national treasure: Assateague State Park (Maryland), Assateague Island National Seashore, and the Chincoteague National Wildlife Refuge on the Virginia side. The Maryland State Park on the north end provides beach access by foot, while the National and Chincoteague parks provide foot- and 4-wheel-drive-vehicle access. All parks offer guarded swimming beaches, camping, and schedule various family activities. Be sure to stop at the Seashore Visitor Center located on Route 611, eight miles south of Ocean City, at the north entrance to the island. The hands-on displays and aquarium are popular with children and adults alike, along with a movie about the ponies on Assateague. On the south end of the island, the Chincoteague Refuge Visitor Center provides information for activities, along with guided walks. Also, a visit to the famous Assateague Island Lighthouse is not to be missed.

There are hundreds of reasons to visit the island, but none so inviting as surf fishing. Fishing off the beach may not have the lure of pursuing the marlin and tuna swimming in the deep, sixty miles to the east, or surf fishing the famed point on the Outer Banks in North Carolina; but, for anyone who enjoys fishing, Assateague surf can be rewarding. This is a great location to introduce children to fishing. There is always something to spark their interest—one minute digging sand crabs for bait or squealing in delights while examining a dogfish shark, the next watching a blowfish double its size.

Everyone enjoys pods of bottlenose dolphin swimming by or observing some of the 300 species of birds that visit the island each year. However, there is a serious side to surf fishing for those inclined. Anglers begin in spring to brave March's cold water/weather and shake off cabin fever by soaking bait for the first striped bass. But April really is the start of the season with stripers and blues arriving in the surf. As the water warms, the variety explodes to trout, croaker, spot, blowfish, flounder, blues, kingfish (whiting), and an occasional pompano.

Five of the estimated 150 ponies on the island make a visit on the beach. There are regulations: no feeding or touching the ponies!

The Ponies

Marguerite Henry's famous book, Misty of Chincoteague, accounts for many visitors to the thirty-seven-mile-long pristine beach each summer. Of course, for local anglers who spend time on the beach fishing, the wild ponies are a common sight. Tens of thousands of visitors come just to see the wild ponies of Assateague Island each year.

Although the ponies have only been on the island for about 300 years, their origins are unknown. Folklore indicates a Spanish ship sank and the ponies somehow made it to shore in a fierce storm. Other stories tell wild tales of pirates bringing the horses to carry all the treasure that was buried on the island and that some of the horses escaped. Whatever the case, the ponies have adapted to the harsh environment and draw a lot of attention. The horses have full roam of the island and may show up anywhere, anytime, and often on the beach. Lucky visitors might even have the opportunity to see them frolicking in the surf. There is a fence at the Maryland/Virginia border that separates the herd in two. In order to control the herd on the Virginia side, during the last week of July there is a pony round up. Cowboys on horseback corral the herd and swim them across the channel at low tide from Assateague Island to Chincoteague Island. This is where an auction takes place for the foals. This controls the size of the herd and provides funding for the Chincoteague fire department. Private boats, along with charter boats with spectators, anchor up to watch the spectacle. Want your own Assateague pony? In 2013, the average auction price was in the neighborhood of $2,000.

Even red and black drum surprise anglers at times, along with the toothy predator of the surf, sharks, which are targeted by many fishermen during hours of darkness (as read in Chapter 6: Beast of the Beach). Fall fishing is exceptional and does not cool off with the water, until the end of November.

There's no shortage of tackle shops while en route to the island's two bridge entrances. A quick stop at any obtains current bite information and bait recommendations. Normally, a variety of offerings such as bloodworms, clams, and squid are all that's necessary. Fresh bunker is a good choice if targeting drum or striped bass, and mullet is great bait for anything swimming in the surf.

Want the best bait possible? Carry a cast net and catch live bait right on the beach. A five-gallon bucket works as a container. Mullet require a lid to prevent them from constantly jumping out. Change the water often or use an aerator to keep bait lively. It is not difficult to cast a net once technique is acquired. Instead of explaining with a series of photos and words, go to the following video link on YouTube where the Fisherman demonstrates the process:

www.youtube.com/watch?v=b0kVOno9pWY

Two of the Fisherman's grandsons find a blowfish and dogfish shark fascinating.

Practice in the back yard until the net opens perfectly. Then, when on the beach, keep these couple tips in mind.

The net needs to be cast upon calm water. The question running through the mind at the moment most likely is, "Where is calm water in the surf?" There is a moment right as a wave comes onto shore when the water is fairly calm or stationary, before water runs back off the beach. In the photograph shown, the net is being timed and thrown so it lands "behind" the wave coming onshore. This is the calm spot, right behind the wave before it breaks.

Depending on time of year, mullet, spot, crabs, and a host of other great bait is available to anglers willing to give a little extra effort for bait collection. Live bait is just about impossible to beat when surf fishing.

Live minnows may get strange looks from some anglers, but flounder devour them in the surf. If targeting flounder, most will be caught close to shore right behind the first breakers.

Flounder like moving bait; casting with a double bucktail rig sweetened with gulp shrimp gets their attention, or a bucktail with minnow combination. Of course, any of the bait caught in cast net will be found appetizing as well. While the flat fish might be anywhere, as mentioned earlier, right behind the breaking waves is a first choice. Standing in the surf and casting parallel to the beach at high tide often puts flounder in the cooler.

Reading the beach is an art learned after spending years watching the surf. Fish may be caught anywhere at anytime along the beach, but the angler who learns to read the water has a great advantage when casting out a line during the end of incoming or first two hours of the falling tide.

The majority of Assateague shoreline descends at a slow rate with just slight depressions. Storms and rough conditions constantly change the bottom contour creating holes and channels, which are prime feeding areas. On bright, sunny days, look for darker-colored water, which indicates depth. The increase in depth is not only identifiable by color, but also by observing how the waves break. Normally, there are two sand bars running parallel to the beach: one within casting distance and one beyond, referred to as the outer bar. The areas between these have slough (deep area) that hold fish. Waves form as water is pushed up on shallow areas or sand bars. Once a wave forms and breaks, white water is visible, as long as it is shallow. When the white water traverses over a hole, drop off, or slough, it disappears and a wave begins to form again, indicating the location to cast a line. It is not necessary to always make long cast. Many anglers actually cast over the fish. A trough sometimes forms within five yards of shore from wave

Another grandson has hands full cranking in fish on a 10'
surf rod, but managed to catch a kingfish for the cooler.

backwash. Although these troughs are almost right on the beach, do not discount them from holding feeding fish during high tide. Small baitfish call this area home and, at times, attract predators right into the whitewash. In the fall, try lures for striped bass at high tide by wading out into the surf and casting down or up the beach, as mentioned, when targeting flounder. Work the lure parallel with the beach in the trough.

Cuts or channels offer one of the best opportunities for bent rods. They form through the outer sand bar creating a funnel bringing an array of fish inshore. To locate, watch waves building and breaking as they come onto the outer bar. When a location is identified where a wave does not break, but consistently tends to build and roll over a section of the bar without white water, mark the spot! Low tide is the best time to observe for cuts and locate these fish-gathering areas. Also watch for riptides, which are formed when water is carried up onto the beach by waves, then finds a weak spot in the bar and escapes back out to sea. Riptides are easily identifiable by a strong, outgoing current; it moves sand and creates a fish-attracting depression or channel.

No surf rods—no problem. As mentioned before, often fish can be caught almost right on the beach. If you have a fishing outfit and enough proficiency to cast 100 feet, you are in business. One day, a young child with a freshwater Zebco 202 in hand was observed catching fish! Although, an eight- or nine-foot outfit spooled with seventeen- to twenty-pound test braided line handles ninety-five percent of fish hooked and often can be cast past the outer bar. If targeting striped bass or red drum, a heavier rod is necessary to throw six to eight ounces of lead and large bait when it is rough.

Unlike many types of fishing, equipment to get started is minimal. A few rigs, bait knife, rag, and bucket to carry everything gets you started. It is beneficial to have a sand spike (three-foot piece of two-inch PVC cut on an angle at one end) to keep the reel out of the sand when baiting hooks or growing tired of holding the rod. But, keep in mind, holding a rod allows the angler to feel the bite, which may be missed when the rod is in a sand spike. Most of the fish are small, so do not use large hooks. A standard double bottom rig with #2 or #4 hooks and a two- to three-ounce pyramid sinker gets the job done. Adjust sinker weight for surf conditions. Provide kids with a light outfit that is easy to handle, equipped with #8 hooks baited with small strips of squid. This rig normally keeps kids busy catching small spot at the surfs edge, which "Dad" can use on a fish finder rig for a trophy Striper!

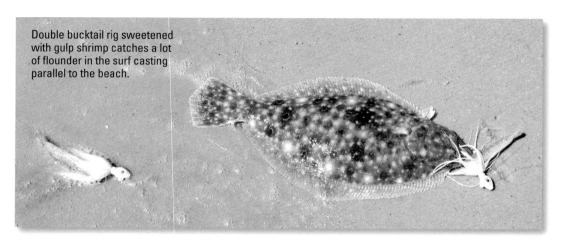

Double bucktail rig sweetened with gulp shrimp catches a lot of flounder in the surf casting parallel to the beach.

Kingfish, when hooked, typically runs in towards the beach. Fisherman's grandson kept slack out of the line and beached this one for the frying pan.

This grandson's "trophy" unfortunately did not meet
minimum length and was released with a frown!

Surf Fishing Tips

- ⚓ **Cast out** and slowly wind back in to locate fish.
- ⚓ **A light east wind** brings fish close to shore.
- ⚓ **Best fishing** is normally at dawn, dusk, or overcast days.
- ⚓ **Use floats** on hooks to keep bait off bottom when crabs are a problem.
- ⚓ **Do not force** large fish to the beach; use the waves to help land fish—just be sure to keep slack out of line.

Assateague Island has camping accommodations at the Maryland State Park, National Park, and in Virginia at Chincoteague. For those who don't want to rough it, Ocean City, Maryland, is a mere fifteen minutes away. A week's pass can be obtained for entrance to the Island, along with a beach pass for driving on the beach.

Assateague Island: certainly the Fisherman's idea of fun in the sun.

The Fisherman's wife worked up a sweat putting this one on the beach. The striper took a live spot on fish finder rig caught in a cut on the outer bar.

Tackled!

- ⚓ **AVAILABLE SPECIES**
- ⚓ **BAIT**
- ⚓ **READING BEACH**

Chapter 28

Ship-Shape Structure

Making use of structure when fishing offshore

Freshwater anglers who fish for largemouth bass certainly understand structure. The same holds true for anglers bouncing bottom for stripers in bay or work inlet jetty rips for blues or sea trout. Both fresh and saltwater fishermen count on structure to put fish in the box—well, at least they count on structure until running offshore and then it is often forgotten. Dropping lines and trolling around a lump or shoal might catch a fish. But locating and taking structure into consideration from the shoreline out to a 500-fathom line when planning where to troll is worth the time and effort. The number one attracting ocean structure is seldom taken into account when trolling: wrecks. They attract more than just sea bass, tautog, and other bottom-dwelling species. The actual number of wrecks that lay on the sandy bottom of the ocean will never be known. But, there are enough to include when laying out a trolling pattern. When trolling offshore, one eye should be dedicated to the sonar, so bottom structure encountered can be saved for further investigation. It is surprising the number of bottom structure the boat encounters when an eye watches the sonar. Leland Downey located 875 wrecks just off the New Jersey coast from Sandy Hook to Cape May.

There was a time when the ability of the NSA could not have obtained wreck numbers from anglers' grasp. Fishermen treated numbers like buried treasure and carefully guarded the secret locations—but not any more. Just about every nautical chart lists wrecks with longitude/latitude and, on old charts, loran coordinates. By joining fishing or diving organizations, wreck locations often can be obtained as well. (In Ocean City, Maryland, the Ocean City Reef Foundation (www.ocreeffoundation.com) provides a list of hundreds of wrecks and structure numbers off the Delmarva Peninsula.)

Wreck locations begin the food chain with growth attaching to the hull. This provides food and shelter for small fish, which in turn attract larger fish, followed by savvy anglers. Trolling around wrecks has saved the Fisherman on more than one slow day of charter fishing. One wreck along the twenty-fathom line even gets credit for putting some green in the pocket when it produced the tournament's winning bluefin tuna. The fish was taken just inside the twenty-fathom line, right on top of the Marine Electric (26942.7 - 42038.5) after inhaling a green machine.

Think of structure as a restaurant for fish. Visitors include tuna, amberjack, wahoo, king mackerel, and other sought-after game fish. When planning a trolling pattern, include wrecks or structure located in the intended fishing area. Troll each piece of structure working against, with, and across the current before moving on to the next location. It is not necessary to drag lures directly over the structure. Pelagic are constantly on the move and will be feeding in the general area. Wrecks can make for some very productive trolling.

Chunkin for tuna around deteriorating bottom structure is also rewarding. Anchor a hundred yards up current. This allows the chunk line to draw tuna from the structure area, while providing room to fight fish. Or set up drifts in the area of structure. Chunkin near structure does not have to occur in the deep to catch pelagic. When running chunkin charters, day after day, out to favorite fishing lumps, several years back, the Fisherman often wondered how many tuna were passed over while running to get "offshore." More than once the thought crossed mind to stop closer to shore and give some edges and wrecks a shot. However, clients probably would not have taken too kindly "trying" to catch tuna, while other charter boats were on a productive lump catching.

One day, the boat was pounding straight into a nasty east wind, which was producing short-stacked waves en route to the recent hot spot where yellowfin were caught the previous few days. As much as the Fisherman wanted to get the charter to the location, it was not worth the beating that the boat, clients, or crew were taking. The boat shut down and set up chunkin at the Twin Wrecks (26971 - 42265) a mere eighteen miles off the beach—a popular location for head boats targeting sea bass. The Fisherman had heard stories over the years from old timers who told of marlin and tuna caught within sight of the Ocean City, Maryland, shoreline. But the Fisherman could never bring himself to tuna fish that close to shore. Seeing high-rise hotels while tuna fishing off the Maryland coast just didn't seem right. Nevertheless, this day proved the rumors correct. The yellowfin were more than cooperative. Since that eye-opening day, the Twin Wrecks and other inshore structure have given up bluefin and yellowfin tuna on occasions. The fish cannot be counted on routinely, as out in the deep; but, there are days when the boat has limited out with less than an hour run.

Man-made reefs, or wrecks closer to shore, should not be discounted in their ability to hold pelagic species as well. The Fisherman can vouch that bluefin can be caught within twelve miles of the inlet at Ocean City. This is not to say a lot of time and effort should be spent every time running offshore to work these types of areas. But considering the current price of fuel, it may be worth the time to check out inshore lumps or structure.

Even before bluefin make their early summer appearance in the mid-Atlantic, anglers will want to fish structure for mako. Set up a drift pattern beginning a mile above a wreck. It is not recommended to break a slick once drifting, so plan the drift to bring you as close to the wreck as possible. Judging the current and wind for the correct drift is not difficult. Watch the GPS when drifting and make adjustments by bumping the engine in and out of gear when necessary. This will allow the slick to stay intact. If anchoring, ignore the wind and set the anchor according to the current. Set up approximately one-quarter mile up current from the wreck. Throw over the chum bucket and draw sharks cruising the wreck area looking for easy meals.

Structure has uses other than bottom fishing. Use it to cash in on game fish as well.

Tackled!

⚓ **LOCATING WRECKS**
⚓ **CHUNKING AROUND WRECKS**
⚓ **TROLLING STRUCTURE**

Chapter 29

Sharks, Camera, Action!

Catch and release tournament shark fishing

The cockpit turned into pandemonium when the mako swam under the boat, surfaced on the opposite side, and spun the wire leader around its body.

"Get the rod tip down deep in the water!" the Fisherman shouted.

The angler thrust the rod tip as deep as possible to keep the line from chaffing on the bottom of the hull. Engines roared, straining to move the boat backwards to clear the line. And, as if this was not enough to raise blood pressure, everyone's pulse exploded (as did the decibel level of yelling) when the mako's head popped out of the water with mono leader across the mouth of razor-sharp teeth.

Over the next couple seconds, lady luck smiled upon the crew. The shark cleared the hull; the leader was gently grasped, raising the mako head a little further out of the water, as a placard containing catch info was placed in view of the camera lens along with the shark. A millisecond later, the only thing remaining at the end of the leader was a hole in the water into which the shark disappeared after shearing through the mono.

The crew's eyes turned towards the bow, where a team member was standing with the tournament camera in hand, who immediately blurted out, "I got it!"

The shouting from crew was probably heard onshore; the catch was called in to the committee boat and four more points were jotted down on the daily release sheet. Welcome to tournament catch-and-release shark fishing.

The Ocean City Shark Tournament celebrated its thirtieth year by giving away big checks to lucky anglers. Catch and Release division was given identical status to the kill divisions. Money was paid equally across the board for first, second, and third place in four categories: Mako, Open (largest thresher or blue shark), Catch and Release, and Bluefish. In addition, five added entry-level Calcutta's ranging from $50 to $1,000 were available in every division for anglers feeling skillful or lucky enough to participate.

Perfect timing of this snapped photo contributed to winning the tournament.

While catch-and-release tournament fishing is nothing new in sport fishing, it has never caught the attention of shark-fishing tournaments. Captain Mark Sampson, tournament director for the Ocean City Shark Tournament, has taken tournament shark fishing to the next level, while still preserving the tradition of hanging tackle-busting sharks on a scale to the amazement of crowds gathered to watch weigh-ins. Why change a kill tournament to include catch-and-release paydays equal to the kill divisions? Mark explained that large offshore fishing boats were able to seek out record-breaking mako, often in the deep of the canyons. The Catch and Release division evens the playing field among all those who enter. It allow anglers fishing off smaller boats an excellent chance of winning, since hammerhead, tiger, thresher, and other species are found inshore, near the twenty-fathom line. Additionally, the Calcutta's create big paydays for those participating in the Catch and Release division, thus generating further tournament excitement.

There was one major change that had anglers concerned: the use of circle hooks. Few participants used circle hooks for shark fishing, including the Fisherman. After the tournament, the majority of those using the hooks for the first time for sharks were sold on their use. Hookup percentage stayed the same as J-hooks.

During the tournament, eighteen sharks were weighed-in, while 146 were released. Federal and state regulations have certainly reduced the number of sharks brought to the scale. But, no doubt, the catch and release made a difference as well. On the Fisherman's team, a decent 150-pound mako was released in order to collect four valuable points. In past years, this shark would have been killed and brought to the scale and, shortly thereafter, find its way onto the grill.

How was the Catch and Release division received? Captain Gary Stamm collected a sizable check for his release efforts. He summed up the feelings of many who participated in the Catch and Release division, "I was unsure at first, but Mark did a great job setting up release procedures. It went very well—overall, a great tournament!" He also added, "He [Mark] leveled the playing field by requiring anglers to estimate a shark's weight when reporting a boated shark." This allowed other teams to release sharks that were not in contention for kill-catch awards. Captain Willie Zimmerman who also collected a check conveyed, "Catch and release is a great idea; it not only adds more ways to win, but more money as well!"

To qualify for release points, a photo must be taken of the catch that clearly shows the type of shark, for identification purposes, since each species is awarded various points. A placard must be in the photo containing boat number, date, and catch number assigned to that shark. Unlike sinking a flying gaff, whenever the opportunity presents itself, coordinating a qualifying tournament photo is a task in itself. However, it is the same for every boat competing and a challenging part of participating in the Catch and Release division. The Fisherman's crew managed to take first-place honors, accumulating twenty-four points over two days of fishing by releasing three tiger, two mako, and two dusky sharks—not to mention losing another mako and tiger before photos could be snapped.

Only time will tell whether catch and release will catch on for shark tournament fishing. But after winning the first catch and release shark tournament…the Fisherman is sold on the idea!

Catch and Release Tips

⚓ **Captain Mark Sampson** is a renowned shark fishing expert. He has been using circle hooks to find clients success on his charter boat, the Fish Finder (Ocean City Fishing Center 410-726-7946) for many years. His bait preferences are fresh over frozen in the following order: tuna, false albacore, bonito, mackerel, and bluefish. He offers this advice, "Typically, a small bait will more quickly and easily be slurped down by an average shark."

⚓ **Captain Willie Zimmerman,** a renowned tuna and billfish expert, did well in the tournament and collected a sizeable check. His advice: fish between the twenty- to thirty-fathom lines and target areas where there is an abundance of bluefish. He recommends setting up drift patterns determined by wrecks, humps, or valleys on the sea floor. He prefers a mackerel or bluefish filet as bait.

⚓ **The Fisherman,** who was lucky enough to win the tournament, swears by live bait. First bait choice is a live bluefish rigged under a kite. If live bait is not available, mackerel or bluefish filet is a second choice. Four rods are used with three baits set in the top one-third of the water column and one deep line targeting threshers.

For additional in-depth information on catching sharks, check out the author's book *Offshore Pursuit* or Captain Mark Sampson's book, *Modern Sharking.*

Chapter 30
Chesapeake Chronicle

History of Chesapeake Bay trolling

On September 10, 1909, *Morone saxatilis*, commonly known as striped bass or rockfish by anglers fishing the Chesapeake, swam the Bay in abundance. Grass beds covered hundreds of thousands of bottom acres in six to ten feet of water providing habitat, oxygen, and water filtration. The Susquehanna River feeding the upper Bay ran crystal clear, creating a wildlife breeding paradise and fish sanctuary unlike any other on the East Coast. However, this date in history is also known for the birth of Captain Ernie Ohler, and in the Fisherman's opinion, one of, if not the best, fisherman to ever bounce bottom in the Chesapeake Bay in search of rockfish.

The Fisherman was blessed to have him as a mentor when learning how to fish the Chesapeake. Unfortunately, Captain Ohler passed a few years back. The last time the Fisherman had the opportunity to spend time on the water with the captain was when Ohler was the spry age of ninety-four. He spoke about days long past and his love of the Chesapeake Bay, while shinning a little light on history seen firsthand.

Captain Ohler (not to be confused with his son, Captain Teddy Ohler) began fishing the Bay in 1927. At that time, hardhead were the choice catch. It was not until a couple years later, after making acquaintances with Captain Johnny James, who owned the *Versata J,* fishing out of Mill Creek in Annapolis, that rockfish became the intended quarry. Early years of fishing consisted of seeking out birds feasting on leftovers from breaking schools of marauding rockfish tearing into schools of baitfish. Once located, casting bucktails or drone spoons filled steel tubs to the max—coolers were yet to be invented.

Ernie and Johnny's fishing friendship developed, as did their fish-catching technique. In the mid-1930s, they perfected the techniques of bouncing bottom and it became the preferred fishing method on the Bay for catching rock. Trolling rods were constructed of bamboo, steel, or beryllium copper. It was not until the late 1940s that excitement erupted over the invention of fiberglass rods and their appearance on the consumer market.

Bouncing bottom was an extremely productive way of placing smiles on faces back then, as it still does today. However, it is a dying art. The Fisherman used Captain Ohler's bottom-bouncing technique for catching rock up until the 1970s, when trolling with in-line sinkers became popular for spring fishing. Then bottom bouncing was used mainly during fall. The youth of today would label the bouncing-bottom technique, as "interactive trolling." It is hands-on—the rod is constantly held and worked, not placed in a rod holder. We are talking about one tired shoulder at day's end!

Captain Ohler was known for the statement, "If your rod is not in your hand, you are not fishing!" His favorite outfit was a seven-foot bamboo rod with a #14 tip (impossible to find today) matched to a Pflueger Capital reel spooled with Dacron line. Wire line came about right after WWII and, according to Captain Ohler, "The addition of wire line for rock fishermen was heaven sent," necessitating less weight to reach bottom. The savvy bottom bouncer, today, should match a seven-foot medium action trolling rod with flexible tip capable of handling twelve or more ounces, teamed up with a Penn 309 reel spooled with braided line. The no-stretch line telegraphs every bump, allowing anglers to perceive or "feel" what is occurring on the bottom. Captain Ohler developed two different bottom bouncing rigs: The double bucktail rig, with its shorter leader, is utilized when fishing on shallow shoals. His standard bottom-bouncing rig is used when fishing depths over twenty feet.

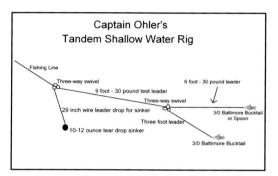

Captain Ohler's
Tandem Shallow Water Rig

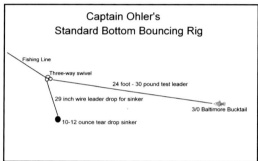

Captain Ohler's
Standard Bottom Bouncing Rig

The two diagrams show using a Baltimore Bucktail. There is no way to estimate the number of Baltimore Bucktail jigs made in Captain Ohler's garage, where lead was melted and countless hours were spent painting and tying real bucktail hair to the jigs. The Fisherman spent several hours on more than one occasion with him pouring lead, producing hundreds of bucktail jigs, and trolling sinkers in various sizes. Normally an eight- to twelve-ounce tear drop sinker suffices for trolling, unless fishing in water approaching thirty feet, whereas sixteen to twenty ounces becomes necessary to maintain a bottom feel.

Captain Ohler's technique for bouncing bottom consists of "feeling" the sinker touch bottom. The rod is swept forward, causing the sinker to leave bottom and resettle in a fish-attracting plume cloud on the bottom. Once bottom is felt, allow the rod to drift back as the boat trolls forward, leaving the sinker momentarily stationary. This allows the bucktail to fall before the process is repeated and it lunges forward, imitating a fleeing baitfish. Properly performed, the technique calls for constantly winding in or letting out line to allow for changing depths. The sinker does not drag on the bottom, but just touches after the rod is swept forward. Once mastered, there is no better way to catch rockfish trolling when fish are schooled up on the bottom, especially in the fall.

Captain Ohler built his own rods and, as mentioned, molded his own "Baltimore" bucktails. He never advised the origin of this small-head bucktail, most popular in a 3/0 or 4/0 hook size, other than to say that Tochtermans, located on Eastern Avenue in Baltimore, was instrumental in the development and marketing of the unique small-head bucktail, commonly nicknamed a "Baltimore."

Captain Ernie Ohler with the fish he loved
to pursue.

Fishing before invention of modern-day
coolers consisted of using a wash tub
to hold the day's catch.

The most popular style was a white head with red crown (wrappings) and white hair. During use, the bucktail was sweetened with a strip of #50 Uncle Josh's pork rind, which is still available for purchase if an angler looks hard. Captain Ohler stressed the importance of splitting the piece of pork rind almost the full length to obtain a "V" shape that provided the correct fish-attracting action. Pork rind has been replaced in most tackle boxes by rubber tails and grubs. However, anglers may want to look to the past and revitalize the use of pork rind when bouncing bottom for greater success. There is a special movement pork rind adds to a bucktail.

The pages on the calendar turned years with consistent Bay rock fishing action from early spring through late fall. Methods included bouncing bottom in the spring and fall, with chumming during the heat of summer, using clams and grass shrimp at locations such as Hacketts Bar, Dumping Grounds, Shallow Shoals, Sandy Point, and the bar off Gibson Island. Fall fishing was especially productive at The Stake, Bloody Point, and the lower Mile Marker off Kent Island. Captain Ohler's records did not show a catch pattern over the years, as fishing was consistently good! Although, he had noted that, in some years, sea trout invaded the Bay and were targeted by using soft crabs as bait. These invasions seemed to coincide with dry summers leading to higher levels of salinity in the Bay.

While the Bay Bridge was still in the blueprint stage (hard to imagine an image of the middle Bay area without the Chesapeake Bay Bridges) when Captain Ohler developed a friendship with Captain Jack Syverson, who owned the *Audry S*. They fished together beginning in 1947 at locations known as Gravelly Run, Hard Bottom, and the shoals at Tolchester. Once the first span of the Bay Bridge was completed in 1952, it did not take long to identify piling number 43 as a consistent producing location, along with the Eastern Shore's rockpile near the channel. It was during this time that drifting eels around the bridge pilings became popular.

Captain Ohler entertained the Fisherman with a few bars of a song, which was routinely sung onboard while fishing. The chorus line, "catch a hundred and go home," tells the story of how many rockfish swam the Bay. Toward the end of the 1960s, after noticing a decline in the rockfish population, most of the Bay captains self-imposed a fifty-fish maximum. Unfortunately, it did not take long for pollution and the disappearance of grasses in the Bay to take its toll on water quality and fish breeding grounds.

It was during this period that Captain Ohler teamed up with Howard Burton and Captain Ray Owen to chase the fish known as the pride of the Chesapeake. Up to this point, most fish caught were for table fare. But a new breed of fishermen was emerging, along with a new Bay Bridge, built 450 feet north of the original and dedicated in 1973. These new "trophy" fishermen changed spring fishing from bouncing bottom to trolling the Bay's channel edges with spoons or large bucktails with inline sinkers in search of spawning rockfish invading each spring. However, even with self-imposed catch limits and additional habitat, such as the new Bay Bridge, rockfish catches continued to decline. A moratorium was imposed in 1985, lasting for four years and landing a blow to the charter fishing industry, along with recreational fishermen. Captain Ohler believed it was the right move and directly responsible for the recovery of the rockfish.

Besides fishing, Captain Ohler did find time to work forty-eight years as an engineer at Black and Decker. In addition, always feeling the need to contribute to the community, for twenty years, he instructed Marine Electronics and Weather courses for the United States Power Squadron, Patapsco River division. Then, in 1998, at age ninety, he decided to fully retire and spend time chasing rockfish on his favorite lumps with his son Captain Teddy Ohler, an accomplished captain in his own right. Apparently, the old adage, "the apple does not fall far from the tree" is correct.

Captain Ohler experienced the Bay in conditions that can only be imagined, catching rockfish in a pristine environment. Unfortunately, he had to watch the deterioration of the water and fish that provided his passion in life. As one of my mentors, I had the distinct pleasure of fishing with Captain Ohler on many occasions. However, he taught more than fishing technique. He instilled the importance of protecting our fragile watershed with everyone who shared a cockpit with him. It is incumbent upon all anglers to protect the Chesapeake Bay and all waters. The Fisherman's life is richer for knowing the man who spoke nothing but good about people: Captain Ernie Ohler.

The photo was taken sometime in the 1940s with Captain Ernie Ohler on the far left, with friends and their day's catch after Sunday church services. Notice the anglers in neck ties, as a sign of respect when fishing on a Sunday.

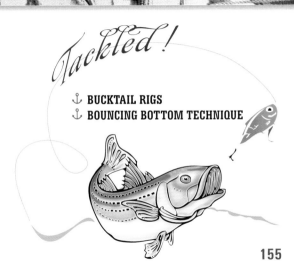

Tackled!

⚓ BUCKTAIL RIGS
⚓ BOUNCING BOTTOM TECHNIQUE

Chapter 31
Black Gold

Sea bass bottom fishing tips

The Atlantic Ocean contains numerous riches for the offshore enthusiast, most notably, billfish, tuna, mahi, and wahoo. For many anglers, a sixty-plus-mile run to the edge of the canyons to find ocean treasure is beyond their boat's ability. Fortunately for these anglers, the inner lumps contain a fortune in black gold, otherwise referred to as sea bass. The succulent fillets of these fish are second to none on the dinner plate, either deep fried or baked. But, just dropping a line to the ocean's bottom does not guarantee dinner will be thrown in the killbox.

Once inshore bottom water temperature warms up to around forty-five degrees Fahrenheit in early spring, sea bass and savvy anglers converge on inshore shoals. The fish are hungry after spending the winter months residing in 40 to 100 fathoms of water from New Jersey to North Carolina. Fishing somewhat slows during the dog days of summer, but comes on strong again in the fall, until cold bottom water retreats the fish back to the deep offshore, where avid sea bass fishermen still target them when the season is open.

Sea bass are a structure fish favoring wrecks, rocks, man-made reefs, jetties, and depth-changing shoal edges—wherever there is food. Smaller fish invade inlets and bays during summer months, but anglers concentrating efforts in cool, deeper water are rewarded with larger bass. Most nautical charts contain GPS numbers for locating artificial reef locations and wrecks for prime action. One valuable source of information often overlooked by fishermen are scuba divers. Speaking from a diver's standpoint, our GPS numbers are dead on. In addition, making friends with a diver can provide an angler important bottom detail. Information such as which direction the structure lies on the bottom is helpful when deciding where to anchor or set up drifts. But, more importantly, divers can advise where on the wreck fish tend to congregate!

Anglers intending to fish off the Maryland/Delaware coast will get a good return on a tax deductible donation of $50 to the Ocean City Reef Foundations (http://www.ocreeffoundation.com). This private organization works hard creating fishing habitat. Financial support is used to purchase structure and construction of artificial reefs. Contributors are provided a list of structure GPS coordinates.

Anglers investing a little time on the World Wide Web before wetting a line may find the time well spent. If fishing Virginia or North Carolina, anglers will want to check out the website www.jimbaughoutdoors.com/gpsdatabase.htm for wreck numbers.

Virginia anglers fishing the mouth of the Chesapeake may also find the site www.mrc.virginia.gov/vsrfdf/reef.shtm helpful.

Jigs are quickly becoming the go-to bait for anglers targeting sea bass.

Using a strip of squid on the hooks of this jig produced a double header of sea bass and blueline tilefish.

Anglers working the waters off the New York or Jersey shoreline will find a good database of numbers at www.jimbaughoutdoors.com/gpsdatabase.htm.

Sea bass can be caught on shoals while migrating or relocating. But, as previously mentioned, dropping lines on a piece of structure is recommended for optimum results. Once structure is located and the sonar indicates the presence of fish, dropping a float should be the next step. The float's line should only be a few feet longer than the water depth. In addition, attaching a highly visible six-foot piece of floating poly line to the float will indicate which direction the current is running. This information is useful for the anchoring process or setting up drift patterns. With the visual float reference set in place over the structure, slowly ride around the area and watch the sonar to identify exactly where fish are located near the structure. It then becomes an easy process to anchor or set up drifts, taking into consideration current and wind by using the float and boat's GPS.

Depending on the piece of structure, anglers may find anchoring the best option to prevent losing rigs, compared to drifting. Sea bass do not feed 24/7; if present, do not give up if they are tight mouthed. Anglers may be required to wait until the dinner bell rings, which often occurs with a current change. Also, resituating the boat just a few feet can make a difference by placing the bait right on the fish.

Keep it simple when it comes to rigging. Sea bass may not be huge, but their mouth and appetite are a different story. A two-hook bottom rig with just enough weight to hold bottom is all that's required.

Create rigs using 3/0 hooks on short leader material to reduce snagging on structure. The use of circle hooks also helps prevent snagging and reduces injury to released fish. Just remember when using circle hooks not to "set" the hook; just raise rod tip and wind. Using slightly lighter leader material for sinker attachment can be a hook saver. Anglers quickly learn that bass are not picky eaters once they decide to dine. Squid, clam, minnow, crab, and cut bait normally are on the menu. A bull minnow teamed up with a piece of squid works well. The minnow keeps the squid fluttering, creating an appetizing meal. Run out of bait? No problem, bass are cannibalistic and will eat their own if cut into pieces. However, anglers running out of bait or preferring to catch larger fish (who doesn't?) may want to consider using jigs.

Many companies manufacture jigs, mainly for tuna fishing, but these jigs work for sea bass. Anglers can be overwhelmed when looking down the jig isle in a tackle shop at all the colors and sizes. But fear not…they all work! Sea bass just don't care what color the jig is; the Fisherman has come to the conclusion that it is the movement that provokes the strike.

There are three ways to rig jigs as shown in the photo: Single hook top, double hook on top, and single hooks top and bottom. The Fisherman normally rigs with two hooks on top of jig. Studies have shown fish attack the head of jigs first. And it works as you can see in this photo where two sea bass were caught on the jig simultaneously. This is not an uncommon catch.

The size of jig depends on water depth and current, but larger bass have no problem inhaling five-, six- or even ten-ounce jigs. Bucktails or diamond jigs find success as well. The new butterfly jigs exceed the Fisherman's expectations. Year after year, jigs out-fish baited lines by a margin of three to one while being responsible for the larger bass thrown in the killbox. Most strikes occur as the jig falls, so be prepared! A first choice jig is the Shimano Butterfly. If the jig does not receive a bite before reaching bottom, immediately begin working it up to thirty feet off the bottom before free-spooling back down and repeating. When bass are

Standard two hook bottom rig and squid is all that's necessary to put sea bass like this in the fish box.

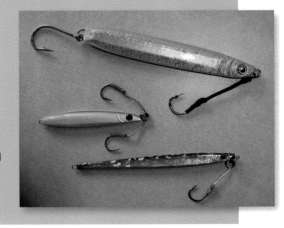

Jigs come in all different sizes and shapes; the good news: they all catch sea bass.

tight lipped, adding a piece of squid to the jig's hook often gets their mouths open.

It should be noted that a wreck or piece of structure can be overfished. When mostly small bass are encountered, it is time to seek out new locations with less fishing pressure. While anglers like to gather all the riches possible, think conservation and keep only the amount of black gold necessary for consumption.

It is common, when winding fish to the surface out of deep water, for the swim bladder (which regulates buoyancy) to expand, causing the stomach to come out of the mouth. This pressure needs to be relieved before the fish is released. Caution: Do not puncture the inverted stomach, this will kill the fish. Anglers can carry a venting tool, which is a thin, hollow-type device. A needle from a hypodermic syringe works or there are commercial devices on the market such as VENTAFISH (www.ventafish.com).

Vent fish by placing the venting tool an inch behind the base of the pectoral fin at a forty-five-degree angle towards the front of the fish. Insert needle just far enough to hear air escape. When air stops, revive fish, if necessary, and release to be caught another day. No venting tool? Wind the fish slowly to the surface; the fish can adjust swim bladder and prevent inversion of the stomach—no need to vent.

The Fisherman does not know the mortality rate when venting a fish with a commercial or homemade-type device; but, the following method is used on his boat instead of venting. It is simple, works, and, in his opinion, is better than venting. Dedicate an old fishing rod as the "release rod." Tie a ten-ounce sinker on end of line along with a 1/0 hook with barb flattened or filed off. On the under side of sea bass, there is a soft piece of flesh. Just barely hook the fish through this.

Lower the fish about thirty feet (marking line helps) and give rod a sharp jerk. As the fish descends, the bladder deflates and, upon becoming free, it swims back to the bottom.

Commercial and recreational fishermen both target this popular fish equally, creating substantial pressure. Nonetheless, Mother Nature has appeared to take this into consideration and has given the species the unique ability to change sex. The majority of fish are born female, allowing egg production until transforming sex to male around the age of three-to-five years.

There is much discussion over the health of the sea bass fishery, with federal regulators feeling the species is overfished. The Fisherman can say for certain that, over the years, it has become necessary to fish further and further offshore to catch quality sea bass.

The Mid-Atlantic Fishery Management Council sets sea bass regulations north of Cape Hatteras, North Carolina. Currently the limit is fifteen fish per day with a 12½-inch size limit.

The South Atlantic Fishery Management Council (waters south of Cape Hatteras) allots five fish per person, thirteen-inch size limit. However, keep in mind fish caught in federal waters are returning to state water; state regulations must be followed.

Buddy of the Fisherman shows off a nice double-header of the delicious, eating sea bass.

Tackled!

⚓ **STRUCTURE**
⚓ **RIGGING**
⚓ **JIGGING**
⚓ **RELEASING FISH**

Chapter 32
Big Dog

For the first few months of life she narrowly survived. Life's tough living in a weed bed, avoiding predators stalking dinner. Fortunately, her species [*Makaia nigricans*] grows quickly and, now, a few years later, the tables had turned, with her being the predator who swam beneath large, floating mats of grass in search of the next meal. In the small world of a weed line, life and death plays out daily. Survival depends on taking refuge in grass anytime a large, dark shadow from below makes an appearance.

Without power of reasoning, the blue marlin was unaware that thousands of miles of open ocean had been covered since those early days of living in a weed bed. Now, life consisted of two things: eating and reproduction. Currently, the marlin was in an area that anglers referred to as Baltimore Canyon.

Keeping a 400-pound body constantly on the move requires nourishment and, up until the recent storm, a weed line several miles long had kept her stomach full each day feasting at the buffet. Great white and large mako were reason for concern; but, other than those two species, she was the big dog on the block. When in feeding mode, her body turned iridescent blue, making even schools of fifty-pound yellowfin uneasy when cruising the area, also looking for dinner. Unfortunately, strong wind and waves out of the northeast recently broke apart the restaurant and scattered it across many miles of ocean. Finding dinner now was going to take more effort.

"What are we fishing for today?"

The charter had booked an offshore trip and arrived at the boat right on time, 4:45 a.m. Like many charters, they had in hand a couple coolers and bags that contained probably most of the clothing that was brought along on vacation.

"Really up to you; yellowfin bite has been pretty good, but with wind last two days, haven't been able to get out. Gonna be a guessing game." As the Fisherman spoke, he stepped out of the boat up onto the finger pier. A hand of greeting was extended as introductions were made on the dock.

Over the next few minutes, the charter's personal items were stored below and it was determined they really didn't care what they caught. None of the six guys had ever fished offshore—just wanted to catch fish in the ocean. It always amazed the Fisherman how many people (not anglers) chartered the boat to go fishing. Apparently, it was just another way to spend a day of vacation, doing something never done before that might be enjoyed.

By 5 a.m., dock lines were cast off and an excited crew was checking out what was to be their home for the day. It was clear they were really planning on enjoying

This stunning view makes a person thankful for breathing salt air.

this one day of vacation without the wives and kids, since everyone reached into the cooler for an ice-cold beer for a toast before the boat even cleared the inlet!

A few miles offshore, bait created ripples upon the ocean's calm surface as the sun began another day for anglers lucky enough to be on private and charter boats heading offshore on this beautiful morning. The sign of life in early morning reinforced the Fisherman's optimistic attitude for the day; it was going to be a good day. The crew seemed pleasant and he hoped the bite held like before the northeast blow. If so, it would be a memorable and enjoyable day for the charter.

The Fisherman's plan was to run back to the Baltimore Canyon where the bite had been going off, since there were no other recent catch reports. Canyons vary in structure and the Baltimore provides anglers an opportunity to fish from thirty down to 500 fathoms by traversing a relatively short area. This can offer a unique opportunity to catch several different species and explains why it was one of the favorite locations for offshore fishing when running out of Maryland, Delaware, or New Jersey. Yellowfin tended to congregate along the fifty-fathom curve, but anglers trolling into the center of the canyon in 500 fathoms often found big eye.

Of course, white and blue marlin found the upwelling along canyon walls to their liking as well. While pelagic fish do not stay in one area all the time, schools of yellowfin had called the Baltimore Canyon home the past few weeks, providing charter boats almost guaranteed catches. Summer had drifted into the dog days of August and calm weather had allowed a large weed line to form, providing a food chain and great fishing. However, with the recent wind, that was sure to be gone.

The boat shut down at the thirty-fathom line and the normal mixed spread was put out for early morning. This consisted of two flat lines, one with naked dink ballyhoo, the other with a medium sized ballyhoo skirted with pink sea witch. One short rigger had a rainbow color spreader bar, the other a medium ballyhoo skirted in a blue/white Ilander. One long rigger had a crystal Ilander skirted over a medium ballyhoo. The other long rigger was run a little shorter, within sight. This line had a large ballyhoo skirted in a dark-colored sea witch. The sea witch hair had been trimmed so it was only about three inches long, allowing the swimming movement of the ballyhoo to be observed by fish. There was a sweet spot line, which was run in the middle of the spread behind the short riggers. This line had a black/purple Iland Tracker skirted over a medium ballyhoo; this was rigged on wire in case a wahoo found it appetizing. No fish in the ocean seems to be as color conscience as the wahoo, who is partial to dark-colored lures/bait. Plus, the wire leader had no effect on yellowfin or bluefin tuna, who also found black/purple lures or bait to their liking. The final line was deployed way back and run off the bridge. This rod dragged triple green machines behind a big green bird.

In addition, two teasers were run off outriggers along with a dredge run off port outrigger. This was the side where the larger baits were deployed in the spread. With the eight line spread in position, everyone sat back and watched baits jumping in and out of a beautiful calm ocean.

The weed line that had been one of the main reasons behind the recent good bite was now just patches of weeds scattered everywhere. There was no way of dragging bait around the patches, and hooks were constantly fouling, creating a nightmare for the mate. He did a great job keeping hooks free of grass and it did not take long until the first fish of the day ended up on ice in the killbox.

A couple more mahi joined the first one. Then the bite slowed as morning turned into afternoon, without any more knock downs. The Fisherman turned the bow to the east and began working into deeper water. Once in 200 fathoms, a large splash was caught off in the distance out of the corner of one eye, but he was unable to tell what it might be. Instinctively, the boat was turned in that direction.

The marlin saw a school of thirty-pound yellowfin near the surface and charged, slashing her bill in hopes of stunning one to fill her now near-empty stomach. It was a miss and she flew out of the water, momentarily entering a strange world, as she had thousands of times in life, before falling back into the ocean. She enjoyed this feeling and often free-jumped for no reason at all. But this jump had a purpose; the yellowfin scattered and she went back on the prowl. Chasing a single tuna was not worth the effort. A few minutes later, she noticed a disturbance on the surface with several small-type fish. The fish were not nearly large enough to fill the void of not feeding the previous day, but a sound was intriguing and she swam up behind one of the fish that appeared to be trying to catch up to a small school.

"Marlin right flat!" the Fisherman shouted down to the mate, but he had been paying attention and already had rod in hand and was free-spooling the pink skirted ballyhoo.

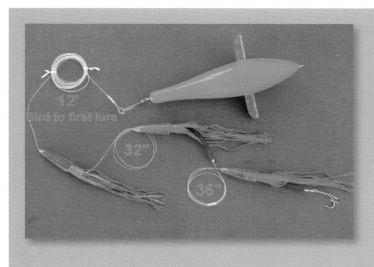

Triple Green Machines rigged behind a bird accounts for many bluefin and yellowfin tuna coming over the transom.

The mate makes another client a very happy angler.

Moments later, the hook came tight and, as line screamed off reel, it was handed off to the angler sitting in the fighting chair. Immediately, the charter started yelling shouts of joy when several spectacular jumps occurred.

The marlin had never felt anything trying to prevent her from swimming and did the only thing she knew when panicked: she swam quickly and jumped. The small fish in her mouth could not be dislodged. Time after time she jumped, but to no avail. Then, as a last attempt, she came out of the water and defied gravity (as only blue marlin can) by swimming in air.

Since jumping did not dislodge the meal, she tried going deep. There was a feeling of security at a depth of 1,000 feet where at times she swam. But on this dive, she sounded only a few hundred feet before some type of resistance held her back. Slowly, despite all effort, she reluctantly rose toward the surface.

The angler was nearing exhaustion; for over an hour, it had been a battle of determination at both ends of the line; finally, it seemed he was getting the upper hand. It was then the angler asked who else wanted to fight the fish, saying he couldn't do it. The Fisherman wanted to get the angler the release and prevented the rod from being handed off, then asked him to hang in there a little longer. The angler shook his head in the affirmative and advised he would try, as sweat dripped off his brow. Several minutes passed until finally the marlin surfaced, slowly swimming away from the boat pulling steady drag off the reel. The top half of the large powerful tail was above water swinging side to side, seventy-five feet behind the transom. Suddenly, engines roared after being thrown into reverse.

"Wind as fast as possible; let's try to get the release!"

The transom lowered under the strain of props chewing at water. Waves splashed against the transom, producing a rain shower on everyone in the pit. Air sucked in under the hull to the props causing cavitation; the boat shuttered and shook. The Fisherman had been in this situation many times; it was possible the fish would make a last-ditch effort to escape and go deep again, but the last thing the Fisherman wanted was for the tired fish to die on the end of the line.

An eighty class outfit would have made all the difference in the world with the amount of pressure that could be applied, but on the fifty class International with an inexperienced angler, success was going to be now or never. The angler was spent and didn't have any fight left in him; luckily, either did the marlin. The wind-on leader came towards the rod's tip as the angler, hunched over in the fighting chair, wound for all he was worth. The mate stretched out, grabbing the leader and confirmed the catch, producing cheering and shouts from the crew. The angler slumped down in the chair with a smile—the Fisherman was not sure if smile was for the catch or not having to wind anymore! The marlin cooperated while being wired and, with bill in hand, the hook was removed and photos were taken. The boat then moved forward as the mate held bill to revive.

⚓ It is important never to take more than one wrap around a hand with fish of this size. More than once mates have been pulled out of the cockpit—unfortunately some to death. Also, it is not recommended to "reach" and be off balance when trying to grab a leader, as the mate was in this situation. Both feet should be firmly planted when wiring a fish. Although they are not used often, anglers targeting large pelagic might want to consider a harness system to keep the mate in boat.

Blue marlin are spectacular at the end of a line, putting on a show never to be forgotten.

Another battle of man against beast ends well for both.

The marlin was fatigued lying on her side trying to replenish oxygen—no strength left to resist the restriction on her bill. Suddenly, the small fish was gone and water ran into her mouth and out gills as if swimming. She could feel energy and quickly felt strength surge throughout her body. A kick of the tail propelled her downwards from the strange experience. A few minutes later she was once again in search of a meal to fill her stomach.

As the charter dug ice-cold beer out of the cooler for a toast, a shout came down from the bridge, "Go ahead, wrap it up."

It was almost 3 p.m. and the Fisherman always liked ending the day on a good note. During the ride back to the marina, there were several more toasts before engines eased into reverse again, this time to back into the slip.

The beer cooler was empty! Six very happy vacationers climbed off the boat; they'd certainly enjoyed one day of their week away from work, catching fish in the ocean!

Pro Thoughts

The Fisherman has had the privilege of fishing with some of the best blue water captains/mates. When a few of these experts were polled on ability of blue marlin to distinguish color, overwhelmingly they were in agreement that color makes a difference—although, they all do not agree on what colors! Here are a few suggestions from the Pros, some who fish all over the globe for blue marlin. Anglers wishing to tangle with the most powerful pelagic that swim the ocean might just want to consider the follow color/bait recommendations from professionals who make a living targeting blue marlin.

⚓ **Captain Josh Ruskey:** Raise fish by using 1656 Black Bart Slant Heads as teasers in the colors of black/purple and black/green; then pitch them a rigged mackerel.

⚓ **Captain Willie Zimmerman:** Match the color of the blue marlin's favorite meal: a dolphin. Skirt a mackerel with a chartreuse Ilander.

⚓ **Professional Mate Jon Meade:** I like pulling horse ballyhoo skirted with a blue/white Ilander or use artificial lures in the colors of black/blue or black/green.

⚓ **Captain Bo Dobson:** Late summer, when targeting 600-plus-pound fish, I pull a large Spanish mackerel skirted with a black/red Hawaiian eye off the short rigger.

⚓ **Captain Mark Radcliffe:** A blue/white Ilander skirted over horse ballyhoo gets a blue's attention.

Chapter 33
Getting Wet!

Thoughts on the wisdom of backing down on fish

The ocean wave came rolling over the transom and, suddenly, the Fisherman was standing in six inches of water in the pit. The scuppers once again were being put to the test. Fortunately, the sliding salon door was closed tight as water sloshed around and splashed up against it. The tracks would need to be sprayed down again with silicon at day's end to prevent corrosion. Underfoot, alarms started going off down in the engine room as pumps kicked on from water flowing down the engine room stairwell. The one-inch, raised, fiberglass edge behind the engine room door in the cockpit did little when water was six inches in the pit. The Fisherman looked up towards the bridge, where the Captain had a big grin on his face; he wasn't the one getting wet! The owner paid no attention to the alarms anymore, since backing down occurred so often.

The white marlin was jumping just a few yards off the transom; finally, the Fisherman got leader in hand and the boat lurched back into forward. Immediately after release, the transom door was opened to let remaining water out of the pit. The owner was smiling and gave the Fisherman a high-five. *There must be an easier way to make a living* crossed the Fisherman's mind as he stood soaking wet.

Boat backs down hard as the Fisherman's nephew winds for all he is worth, as the mate waits to get hands on leader and confirm billfish catch.

There is no denying the adrenaline-rush experience (anxiety?) when a wall of water washes over the transom combined with aerial billfish. Is there an appropriate reason or time for the bilge pump test maneuver or do captains only use reverse for show? Or maybe the question should be: Is backing down seventy miles off the beach responsible? Certainly, affirmatively, positively, definitely, absolutely, without doubt…NO!!! Then why does it occur? Well, in the situation described here, the owner wanted to release as many white marlin as possible when a bite was going off; backing down added to release numbers faster and allowed more bragging rights around the Tiki Bar at day's end. And yes, another reason boats back down is probably due to captains just liking to make everyone wet in the pit to put on a show. (The Fisherman has actually been accused of this!)

There are legitimate reasons for backing down. A transom moving south and pelagic heading north with a full head of steam often causes diesels to go into reverse to prevent getting spooled. Multiple hookups cause chaos in the pit and is another time water often comes over the transom. Two fish going different directions makes for an interesting situation and, often, the boat backs down so line can be recovered from both fish at the same time when the opportunity presents itself. When a billfish is swimming just off the transom, backing down allows the leader to get into the mate's hand, without the angler needing to fight the fish closer to the boat.

Now, with everything previously stated, keep in mind there are other options. Working a fish by running a thirty-degree angle in the direction of fish in order to recover line is the first option. It is awkward fishing out of the side of the boat when sitting in a fighting chair or even with knees against side of boat with stand up gear and fish pulls rod towards bow, but it is an alternative. A boat running parallel to a fish to regain line is the only option for outboards, or at least it should be. The splash well of outboard boats was never developed to handle the amount of water created when a boat backs down. Even with a full transom, consideration on backing down with outboards hanging on the back or inboards needs a lot of thought before engines are pulled into reverse. The Fisherman has only observed a handful of boats designed with what he believes are scuppers large enough to remove hundreds of gallons of water quickly enough. This amount of water can come over the transom in mere seconds when the boat is in reverse and meets an unexpected, rising swell or wave. Once that amount of weight is in the boat, the next wave coming over can be catastrophic. It is one thing to have a thirty-ton boat handle an additional ton of water on deck, but quite another for a twenty-six footer to do the same. An option for an open bow boat is to actually chase the fish and fight it from the bow area. Many boats have a chair mounted in the bow for this. At the very least, the angler can sit on a cooler with belt and harness in bow area. More than one boat has ended up full of water due to backing down while trying to save a fish and ended up as structure on the bottom of the ocean. Of course, the ability of the boat, captain, crew, and sea conditions dictates whether backing down can be accomplished safely.

Better to catch a fish or save the boat to fish another day? Your choice!

Backing down is an adrenalin rush, but is it responsible?

Fishing is fun, fishing is fun, fishing is fun…sometimes we need to be reminded in situations like this!

Chapter 34

Tips & Tricks of the Trade

Making life easier for the offshore angler

The difficult made easy—happens in all walks of life—little things that save time or make a task easier. Believe it or not, even fishing can be made simpler and more fun. After countless days of fishing over the last fifty years, the Fisherman has picked up a few ways to make the routine...simpler.

Take something like **cleaning the boat** for example. Blood cleaned up immediately after fish hits deck saves a lot of scrubbing once back at the dock after it dries. Not talking about just throwing a bucket of water on the deck, but actually washing under the gunwales, cooler lid, etc., saves a lot of time back at the dock after blood dries.

How about **maintaining the outside of the hull**? Anyone who tries to keep the outside of the hull sparkling clean knows this can be an issue. One area of scrubbing that is necessary on the hull is where water runs off the boat when washing down at day's end or when the boat takes spray and runs down gunwales from the bow. Sometimes, just thinking a little outside of the box saves elbow effort—such as a piece of plastic screwed under the rub rail. This prevents water from running down the side of the hull causing hard-to-remove stains. Yeah, the designer of the boat maybe should have thought about this, but the Fisherman's guess is he never set foot on a boat.

Unless outriggers are equipped with a locking-down device, weight of lures/bait causes **creeping down of the lines**. A simple fix is using a long line clip. This one-dollar investment stops the need to constantly raise lines back up to end of riggers. Use a couple crimps and foot-long piece of 200-pound mono to keep clip ready for use. Being stainless steel, there is no worry about rust creating marks on gel coat.

Speaking of creeping, **drag on flat lines when billfishing** needs to be almost non-existent. Trying to set reel drag at this level is somewhere near the difficulty of putting excess toothpaste back in the tube. Line slowly creeps out, especially when in waves. And more often than not, the person responsible for constantly resetting the line doesn't pay attention and, suddenly, 200 yards of line is off the reel. Using the reel clicker is not recommended; after a marlin picks up bait and starts running, anglers do not want that clicker noise transmitted down line and clicking in the fish's mouth causing a drop bait. An easy fix is twisting the fishing line several times before inserting in release clip. Just set release clip to extremely light, so it releases as soon as bill swipes bait.

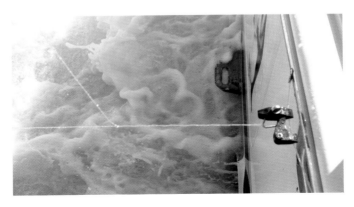

Changing rigs during course of day occurs when there is a slow bite and, by day's end, many rigs have been used to entice a bite. Of course, **once the rig hits saltwater, it needs to be washed at the end of the day**. For the most part, a five gallon bucket is used for rig storage during the day on many boats, and this works. However, often back at the dock, there is a large tangle in the bucket that someone has to straighten out while washing. A simple device is made from a piece of pool noodle cut to fit on a plastic hanger. Do not make a straight cut in noodle for inserting hanger; instead, cut noodle in a circle pattern from end to end, similar to a spring. Then the piece of noodle will not fall off hanger under weight of lures. Embed hooks and at day's end, tangling will be at a minimum.

In addition **the lures/rigs can be washed** right on the hanger and hung to dry. The pool noodle idea also works great when wrapped around any one-inch tubing on a boat—on the windshield tubing, top structure support poles, etc. What to do with lures during a day of fishing on small boats just got easier.

There are at least three days each fishing season the Fisherman dreads. This is when **line needs to be changed** on a dozen reels, with each holding hundreds of yards of line. Pulling line off an eighty class reel by hand is a reel pain (yeah, that pun intended). To ease the job, take an old line spool and cut as shown in the photograph. Photos are self explanatory: once spool is full of old line, unbolt, and line comes right off to be taken to tackle shop for recycling.

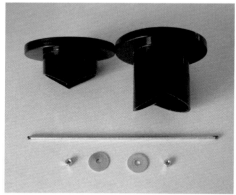

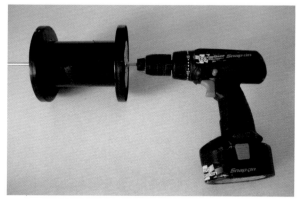

Of course **line needs to be put back on the reels**. If anyone has tried to hand-wind 8,000 yards of line on reels in a day, they know why the Fisherman recommends using the drill and reel connection that was discussed in Chapter 25 for winding in way way back lines when trolling for bluefin. The system works great for spooling fishing reels. Spooling line is really a two-person job, since reel should be spooled under pressure, but can be accomplished by one person. Place new spool of line in a bucket of water and place a wet rag on top. Tension can be adjusted by adjusting the amount of water in the bucket. Spooling reels just became only half the pain it use to be.

174

A cordless drill with connection for reel handle is used for winding in way back lines. Can also be used to simplify process of spooling fishing reels.

Anyone who spends any amount of time offshore is going to foul a prop. The best set of eyes can miss something floating on or just under the surface. This is when a **decent mask** comes in real handy. Opening eyes in salt water is like...well, there isn't anything else like it. It burns and a person cannot see.

Boat props unfortunately find unwanted items in the ocean. The mate took care of this day's inconvenience and fishing continued.

In addition, an extremely **sharp knife** needs to be onboard. The term sharp means "SHARP." Not talking about the bait knife. Holding breath under the boat while exerting a lot of energy cutting means for most people, maybe thirty seconds of cutting per dive. The person performing this task wants/needs a sharp knife. It also makes stabbing that ten-foot mako easier (just kidding…maybe!). Store a thick blade knife (not filet knife) onboard that will not break under the pressure needed to cut heavy nylon rope, and keep knife just for this occasion.

The Fisherman can attest that it is extremely difficult to cut through nylon rope used to pull trawler nets or what seemed like miles of long line wrapped around the prop and strut. The mask and sharp knife is the difference between a pain in the rear or disastrous day requiring a tow (ever… wait…sixty miles off the beach for a tow?). Murphy's Law says this fouling will occur on a rough day and Murphy is seldom wrong. But even on a calm day in gentle seas the boat moves up and down more than can be imagined when underneath. Warning: always have a firm handhold on a shaft or part of the boat so the body moves with the boat in swells. Otherwise, there is a real possibility of serious head/neck injury as boat strikes head.

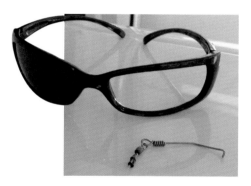

Flying missiles in the form of snaps can cause serious eye injury if not wearing eye protection.

And while we are discussing head injury, anyone working the pit handling the chore of wiring fish needs to **wear sunglasses**—not because the sun hurts eyes on bright days, but on more than one occasion, it has saved a serious eye injury when a snap broke or piece of terminal tackle just decided to give way and flew back right at an eye. Take it from the Fisherman, you cannot move fast enough to get out of the way!

Finally, a rigging tip for circle hooks. One of the biggest complaints the Fisherman hears anglers grumbling about is not being able to **skirt ballyhoo for color presentation like J-hook rigs**. The photo tells the story; anglers can still skirt using a rubber squid. Cut a small hole with a pair of scissors or knife before sliding over the ballyhoo. Then insert circle hook through knot in "X" on top of ballyhoo head (see rigging for circle hooks in Chapter 8). This way, a skirt can be utilized; just match size of skirt to ballyhoo. Sometimes it is necessary to cut off the top of rubber squid and let the nose of ballyhoo stick out—depends on skirt size. Anglers may have to play with this rigging technique to get ballyhoo swimming correctly, but it can be done without an engineering degree and helps catch fish on some days!

Chapter 35
Captain Bligh

Typical day of offshore charter fishing!

The Fisherman walked into the marina's restaurant at 4:10 a.m. It was easy to pick out anglers chartering: their tables were bursting with energy, excited about the upcoming day offshore. He exchanged pleasantries with captains and mates sitting at tables grasping cups of coffee like newfound gold that hopefully cleared the cobwebs. Every fishing season was different, yet every one the same. The day before provided clientele a great bite with killboxes full of bluefin. Crews and charters were in high spirits at day's end and "one more round" at the Tiki Bar tended to be a little later than normal. It was clear a few were paying the price for the partying. The door opened and shut constantly as young mates and new captains rushed in, ordered a breakfast sandwich, and ran back out...only to return ten minutes later and quickly stuff egg and sausage sandwiches into their mouths. This group hurrying were the same people each morning, always tying up loose ends before charters arrived.

In the back corner sat a few retired captains at a big, round table. After a lifetime on the water, they were conditioned to wake up early and still came to the marina at 4 a.m. each morning as a ritual. The Fisherman often wondered about all the knowledge sitting at that table. These captains would answer questions, but never went into the details of how they caught fish routinely. They found no reason to sit with those still fishing—been there, done that, didn't need to hear new stories—would rather reminisce about the old times.

Another table consisted of seasoned captains, the "radio yakers." Anyone who spent twelve hours everyday on the water could close eyes and pick out each VHF voice, since they never shut up all day. They had a tight click and refused to share information, except within their tight, inner circle. Many who sat at this table came off as arrogant to the Fisherman, although not all.

Then there was the "seniority" table. It was an unwritten rule: no one sat down at this table until they "paid their dues," which meant getting at least a couple years of chartering under the belt. Surprisingly, one morning, a captain or mate walking up to the counter would suddenly be invited to join the table. It was never discussed, but conversation normally went something like; "John over there has been catching fish this year." "Yeah, pretty decent guy, good fisherman." Then someone would yell over, "Hey, John, why don't you pull up a chair." And just like that, they became a member of the click. This meant everyone sitting around the table would share fishing location information for the day. And if someone discovered a technique that put an extra fish or two in the box the day before, the new invitee got the scoop. Some at this table had been chartering for over thirty years; the Fisherman pulled up a chair next to the captain he was currently working with.

The captain was in his late fifties and a good fisherman. Presented a nice image: always clean shaven and a neat, pressed shirt. The boat had a lot of charters on the book at the beginning of each year with repeat clients. The captain was a go-getter. Once back at dock after a long day offshore, he quickly washed up and changed into a clean, pressed shirt. Evenings were spent working hard, drumming up charters around the Tiki Bar from people who stopped by to watch fish get weighed in at day's end. He was a good salesman and filled in open days; the boat had very few lay days. His gentle smile and easy-going, mild-manner talk convinced anglers his boat was the one to bet on when it came to catching fish. But like a lot of captains…he had a dark side and was obsessed with catching fish. The number one thing that accounts for getting charters is catching fish and throwing them on the dock for spectators to see at day's end.

At 4:45 a.m., the waitress was told to add tip and put breakfast on the boat's tab as the Fisherman and captain left to walk down the dock to meet the charter. The Fisherman always rigged the night before; only thing to do in morning was call the office on VHF and say how many forty-pound bags of ice the dockhand needed to bring by golf cart and drop off at the boat. Extra preparation in the evenings made for relaxing mornings, even if it did mean missing an hour of sleep occasionally when dragging a tired body to bed after an especially long day offshore. Running around like a chicken with its head cut off in the mornings ended years before.

The captain met this day's charter at the Tiki Bar earlier in the week. They had never been offshore fishing, but thought it might be an enjoyable day after seeing all the bluefin come to the scale that evening. There is nothing like a good bite to peak interest in chartering, not to mention a few libations! Once being assured it would be a great day of vacation, they forked over a deposit. There were four anglers: three men and a woman.

Shortly after introductions and gear stowed aboard, the boat was running upon gentle seas, along with most of the fleet towards what had been a great bluefin bite the past couple days. It was going to be a long ride, almost sixty miles needed to be covered on the run south. A few miles down the beach predawn broke to the east. It caught the charter's attention, who commented about the good luck and fortune that must lay ahead of them this day…little did they know.

During the ride out, the anglers were given instructions how to handle the rod to put fish in the killbox: no jerking rods, no thumbs on spool, be easy working fish, and conserve energy. Fish would be fought in standup gear and it was not going to be easy, since it was going to take on average forty-five minutes to an hour to land the nice class of fish currently being caught on fifty-pound fluorocarbon leaders.

Finally, the throttles pulled back and chunkin began at a location known as Lumpy Bottom, off Virginia, drifting along with five dozen charter boats out of Ocean City, Maryland; Wachapregue, Virginia; and Chincoteague, Virginia. It did not take long until first bite bent a rod over. With rod in hand, the angler got excited, reared back, and snapped off fish.

Then, from up on the bridge, "What the hell! Don't jerk on a fish like that, etc. etc. etc.!" Yelling tapered off to unintelligible words that certainly could not be found in Webster's dictionary.

The angler looked at the Fisherman with a blank stare, before glancing back up at the bridge where the captain had turned around with binoculars in hand, still mumbling. Clearly, this was not the man he'd met at the Tiki Bar a couple nights earlier who laughed, joked around, and was so pleasant. The Fisherman

Every angler on every boat running offshore has the same hope every morning as the sun rises: the hope of catching fish!

A lot of freezer space is required when 400 pounds of bluefin is hanging on the scale. Freezing tuna in bags of water prevents freezer burn and preserves flavor.

assured the angler that snapping off fish occurred routinely with this size bluefin and not to worry about it; just try to keep calm on next fish.

The woman was up next. It did not take long before the chunk of butterfish on the handfed line was inhaled. The fish ran off 100 yards of line before bend came out of rod and slack line fell upon the water. The woman cranked as fast as humanly possible, but there is no way to recover line as fast as the tuna was swimming. Unbeknown, the tuna made a U-turn and was now in front of the boat. Suddenly, the slack line came tight, spinning the woman around who was harnessed to the rod. The rod hit the outrigger and line snapped.

No doubt boats close by heard the Captain's rant, "You have to wind faster; no need to lose that fish etc. etc. etc.!" Once again his voice trailed off to muttering as he turned around shaking head in disgust. The Fisherman assured the woman she did nothing wrong, explaining it's impossible to wind fast enough to keep a tight line with tuna charging the boat.

Another tuna was hooked and after a long, hard battle, and the first fish of the day was gaffed and hit the deck. From up on the bridge Dr. Jekyll offered a word of encouragement. But as the day progressed, whenever a fish was lost, Mr. Hyde emerged and reared his ugly head.

Fortunately, the bite was good and, despite losing a few fish, the daily limit of four bluefin were obtained, averaging between eighty and 100 pounds.

At the scale, the crew's catch was top boat and drew a lot of *oohs* and *aahs* from the crowd that gathered around to admire the fish. As the Fisherman was taking photos of the charter with their catch, the smiling captain with pleasant voice was working the crowd, looking for a charter to fill in a vacant day later in the week. After photos, one of the anglers handed the Fisherman his tip for the day and thanked him for all the hard work. He also asked, "Is Captain Bligh like that all the time?"

The Fisherman shook his head and stated, "No, most of the time, a lot worse!"

Chapter 36
Don't Think!

Turning bites into hooked up fish

Imagine...a beautiful, clear, blue sky, one- to two- foot swells rising and falling in front of a light southeast breeze. The boat approaches a weed line forming along the east wall of the canyon. On horizon, shearwaters are everywhere, displaying command of the air by gliding with wing tips barely off water. A flock of storm petrels exhibit a water dance while picking at oil droplets—that's all that remains from the savage attack upon a school of baitfish right before arriving on scene. Inhaling deeply, the aroma of fish oil upon the air is savored. The atmosphere is fishy, very fishy. Anticipation mounts as each bait is visually checked and rechecked for that pointy, long-billed rascal or another pelagic in the area.

The crew senses the moment. The previous nonstop jabbering has turned to silence; all eyes are fixed on the task of watching the spread. Attention is drawn to the port short rigger where a submerged bally emits a smoking stream of bubbles. It flies out of the water, creating a heart-stopping moment before reentering with enticing movement. Peering down at the dredge in the dark-blue water, you begin mumbling under breath.

"Is that a fish? Shadow? Could swear I see something...*POP!*"

The starboard flat line goes off! If an angler must think what the next step is, chances are he or she may chalk up another missed opportunity. Offshore trolling calls for action, not thinking (at least not on the bite). The process of setting a hook with billfish, or any other species for that matter, needs to be instinctive. The knack is developed through experience. Anglers without this experience should prepare mentally to increase chances of success until knowledge and experience can be gained. The next time opportunity comes knocking at the transom, be prepared.

Offshore anglers enjoy pursuing all types of game fish. However, none captures the desire or imagination that a marlin does behind the transom and no other species offer more of a challenge to hook. There's no time to ponder on what the next move is when a bill presents itself. A game plan needs to be thought out and explained to the crew before lines are set. Billfish are a fortunate encounter for many when trolling offshore for tuna, wahoo, or dolphin. But if an angler wants to catch billfish, attention to the spread is imperative to increase chances. Fishing on slow days makes it difficult to stay attentive toward the spread. When fish are far and few between, this is not the time for everyone to sit around on the bridge with feet propped up. Be in the pit near the rods watching. Anglers can be asleep and still manage to hook-up tuna or dolphin when the drag sounds off, but a marlin will not be that forgiving.

If your normal trolling spread is like the Fisherman's, there is a mixture being pulled in the wake. His spread is a buffet for whatever swims in the ocean, unless the charter indicates strictly to target a specific species. Memorizing what bait is on each rod is essential. It assists in split-second decisions. Billfish appear slapping bait when least expected. Immediately, the bait must be snatched away or dropped back, depending on what is being pulled. It's almost impossible to hook up a marlin on an artificial without visually seeing the fish to set the hook. Fishing on days with a lot of white water make watching baits difficult. To increase chances of catching a marlin, use natural baits on lines that cannot be observed. Missed strikes on these lines can immediately be dropped back, possibly producing a pick-up. It is common for an aggressive billfish to quickly jump from bait to bait. Other times, when billfish are picky, an angler may only get one shot with no time to think about what bait is on that line and how to set up on the fish. Develop a system to reduce confusion that delays action. On choppy/rough days, try natural bait on both long riggers and lines on the starboard side of the boat, leaving artificial lures on visible port lines. This method is simple and easy for a crew to remember. Or using all natural or all artificial bait removes the decision for how to set the hook.

Recalling what baits are on which rods is only half the battle when billfishing. Knowing which bait goes with which rod is the other half of the equation. Seven, eight, or more lines behind the boat can become confusing. Someone screaming "Fish!" from the bridge does not help those in the pit. The crew must be attuned to the same system for efficiency. Numbering the rods is one method. Terms using rod positions, such as port short rigger, starboard flat line, etc., is another great method. However, those not familiar with boat/fishing terms have difficulty with this technique.

Look as you reach! Visual confirmation of what's happening at the bait will dictate next move. When slow reacting to marlin on natural bait, hit free-spool and drop back before lifting the rod out of the holder. This move saves a split second, which can be the difference in a pick-up or swim away. If the bait is not picked up, raise rod over head, wind, and get bait back on the surface even if the fish cannot be observed. If the fish is on an artificial, it may be prudent to begin winding the lure from the fish before lifting the rod out of the holder. This gives time to prepare for dropping the lure back on the next attack. To hook a marlin on an artificial, raise the rod tip and pull the lure away; as the fish attacks the bait he will open his mouth. Lower the rod tip placing the lure in his mouth. When pressure is felt set hook. Do not give the fish time to spit the lure. In either situation, looking at the bait before removing the rod from the holder can save fractions of precious seconds and dictates action.

Turn mystery bites into hook-ups. Often, strikes occur when the head is turned to speak with someone or look at different bait. When a rod is hit and missed, react. It's amazing someone standing next to a rod says he missed it without picking the rod up. If the marlin is not observed with a visual check, pick the rod up and give a couple quick jerks to artificial lures or drop back a natural bait; then, wind with a jerk motion. This will often lure even a tuna or Dolphin back on bait. If mahi are observed missing the bait, winding quickly many times will provoke another attack. If it is a swing and miss on the billfish, do not assume the fish left the area. Often the billfish is below following the baits. Adding additional action to the bait by grabbing the line and jerking can invoke another attack, giving a second chance at catching the trophy.

Want to catch a marlin, stay in the pit, pay attention, and, when that elusive billfish rises to bait, take action!

Is there any image that captures an angler's imagination more than a billfish behind the transom…doubtful!

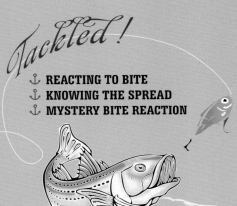

Tackled !

⚓ **REACTING TO BITE**
⚓ **KNOWING THE SPREAD**
⚓ **MYSTERY BITE REACTION**

Chapter 37

Fly a Kite

The art of fishing with a kite

Near the top of the *how to catch fish* list are the words: "bait presentation." The term relates to the swimming ability and appearance of natural bait/ lures. Want to enhance a typical trolling spread and add a new twist to bait presentation? Then go fly a kite.

A kite requires constant attention and fishing with it is a hassle. Then why do anglers use them? That's easy...kites catch fish! Live bait dangling vertically into the water when drifting for tuna or sharking is productive, even more so when trolling rigged bait/artificial lures skipping off to the side of the boat on smooth water. Presenting bait outside the wake, away from boat, can only be accomplished by using a kite.

When the Fisherman first began using kites offshore, they were constructed of cotton. After coming in contact with saltwater, they needed to be washed thoroughly and dried before use again—not to mention mildew being a problem. Fishing kites today are made of new fibers, such as ripstop nylon, and are even capable of flying after falling in the ocean. A quick spray of freshwater and a few shakes is all it takes and the kite is back in business. Aftco, SFE, and Bob Lewis all produce quality kites. BlueMarlinChronicles.com even produces a spar less parafoil kite. (The Fisherman has not tried it, but at $40, this might be worth consideration.)

Kites are sold according to the amount of wind they handle successfully while staying aloft. Depending on the manufacturer, adjustment of where the line attaches to the kite's bridle allows for changing wind speed, or the spars may be changed for wind conditions. The Fisherman uses an Aftco fishing kite ($80), which comes with two sets of spars, allowing the kite to fly in four-to- fifteen MPH winds. The SFE kite ($120) handles various wind conditions from five-to-twenty-five MPH by adjusting the bridle system.

Following the directions for the type of kite purchased all but assures success. It is necessary to dedicate a rod for the purpose of flying the kite. A short rod equipped with a 4/0 reel is a good setup. Braided line does not absorb water like monofilament and is a better line choice; thirty-pound braid line is adequate. One or more lines may be fished off a kite.

The kite rod is rigged in the following manner: For use with one line, insert a barrel swivel 100 feet from the end of the fishing line. A small wind-on-type swivel is necessary, since it must be wound onto the reel. A small Spro or stainless steel Billfisher Krok swivel works well. Then slide on a release clip, such as an Aftco Goldfinger. Finally, a small snap swivel is attached to the end of the line for kite attachment. When deployed, the kite is let out 100 feet, at which point the swivel catches the release clip. Attach fishing line to the release clip and let the kite line and fishing line out at same time to the desired distance from the boat (this is a two-person job). In order to fish two lines on a kite, two different size swivels are used. First drill out the holes on one of the release clips, which allows a small swivel to pass through. Rig the system by inserting the larger of two swivels 150 feet from the end of the line. This swivel will not go through the drilled-out release clip. Then insert the small swivel in the line seventy-five feet from the end of the line, followed by the drilled-out and then unaltered release clips. Attach a quality, small snap swivel to the end of the line for kite attachment. When in use, once seventy-five feet of line comes off the reel, the first small swivel passes through the drilled-out rigger clip, but catches the unaltered clip to carry the first line aloft. After another seventy-five feet of line comes off the kite reel, the larger swivel catches the drilled-out clip to carry the second fishing line from the boat.

The release clip on left in photo (clip closest to kite rod) has been predrilled with a hole large enough to allow the clip to slide over the small swivel. This swivel is seventy-five feet from the kite and passes through this first clip; however, it will catch the second clip (right clip in photo), which will be used to carry the first fishing line away from the boat. A second, larger swivel is tied at 150 feet and will catch the predrilled clip for a second fishing line.

The setup may be used to fish while anchored, drift fishing, or trolling, with wind the controlling factor. A third line may be fished off the kite by using three different sized swivels and appropriate sized holes drilled out in release clips.

Bait presentation when kite trolling allows bait, as mentioned before, to dance or skip on smooth water, which at times is found irresistible by fish. A point that must be remembered when trolling is that there is no turning around! The kite is dictated by wind, not the boat. The boat may come off the wind, placing the kite at a ninety-degree angle to the boat; this angle may be pushed further on windy days. But anymore than ninety degrees to the wind begins to place the boat's movement in the direction of the wind—meaning: the kite does not stay aloft. If trolling circles on a particular lump or edge is the plan for a day of fishing, leave the kite in storage. However, if most of trolling can be against the wind working an edge, the kite may be the ticket for filling an empty killbox.

When large fish are hooked, requiring the boat to assist in landing, it is prudent to wind the kite rod in first. This allows the boat to maneuver in any direction. Either rigged bait or artificial lures may be trolled off a kite. Tuna and dolphin inhale bait, snapping the line free on their first run. Billfish, on the other hand, often slap at the bait with the bill. Since there is a lot of slack in the line, do not wait on the billfish to snap the line from release clip. Free-spool the line while in the rigger clip. Once the fish swims off and increases the rate of line disappearing from the reel (about five seconds) set the hook. This does not allow for a hard set, but is often adequate for the initial strike and can be followed by a second setting of the hook when the line comes tight. Circle hooks and kites work well together, since all that is necessary is winding the line after the bite to set the hook. Tuna find bait jumping out of the water very enticing—raising the rod tip up and down or pulling on the fishing line by hand to create flying bait. If tuna are not feeding on the surface, but observed on the fish finder deep, creating additional movement a couple times every thirty seconds is a trick for pulling the tuna towards the surface to feed. Tuna attack the bait just as it comes off the surface of the water; airborne tuna are a thrilling sight. The kite creates bait action that cannot be duplicated with outriggers.

The Carolina Yummee Fly-n-fish are ideal for kite fishing since it is the only way to make the flying fish lure appear natural. Try trolling the Yummy in the following fashion. Position the boat so the kite is off to one side of the boat and the Yummy is running in clean water. Turn the boat into the wind, then across wind. This quickly places the kite from one side of the boat to the opposite and speeds up the bait, making it skip and fly across the surface. At times, this drives yellowfin tuna wild. This technique is also effective when using rubber squid, which appears to be jumping out of the water. Bait should be in the air fifty percent of the time when targeting yellowfin tuna.

Live bait splashing and swimming around on the surface is the ticket to a memorable day of offshore fishing as well. No leaders for fish to shy away from, just enticing bait. The type of bait to use is limited only by what is available swimming in the fishing grounds. Mullet, goggle-eyes, blue runners, menhaden, pilchards, spot, and cigar minnows all produce results. Rig these live baits using a hook of appropriate size and hook through the back or through the top of the eye sockets. Large bait needs to be bridled. Live bait swim in circles when held by a kite. A quality ball-bearing swivel must be used between the leader and fishing line to prevent twisting. It is also beneficial to attach a piece of bright ribbon where the swivel is located. Swivels are almost impossible to see when 150 to 200 feet from the boat. The ribbon allows anglers to see how much leader is in the water and how deep bait is swimming. When using multiple lines off the kite, it is recommended spacing at least fifty- to seventy-five feet apart. This distance can be tightened up for bait presentation, but care must be taken to keep bait separated far enough to prevent creating a tangled mess. When chunking for tuna on the drift, use a kite and place two additional lines up-wind of the boat. When sharking, try bridling a live bluefish and suspend under the kite for irresistible mako bait. It takes on average three bites for a 150-pound Mako to eat an eight- to ten-pound bluefish. Do not be in a hurry when setting the hook!

Kite Tips

One angler needs to be given task of monitoring the kite. A kite down in the water requires winding in all lines and backing down to retrieve (a real pain in the a#&). Always keep an eye on the kite when flying out to the side of the boat or while attention is diverted fighting a fish.

Launching a kite can be tricky, since the boat creates swirling wind, making getting the kite in the air frustrating from the cockpit. Launch the kite from the bow or flying bridge to reduce problems associated with wind issue.

Flying a kite—it's not just for kids!

Tackled!

⚓ **RIGGING FOR FLIGHT**
⚓ **TROLLING**
⚓ **SETTING HOOK**
⚓ **PRESENTING BAIT**

Chapter 38
Fishing Rough Water

Is it worth the effort?

All week long, when checking offshore fishing reports on the Internet, fish were practically jumping in boats. Weather was ideal, with bright, sunny days accompanied by light winds. Phone calls were made and an excited crew was chomping at the bit for the Saturday trip. Weather forecast was checked a couple times every day, and every time it appeared luck was finally on our side.

Friday evening, a couple dozen ballyhoo were rigged and gear loaded on the boat. One last time the forecast was checked and looking good at SE 5-10; it was going to be a fantastic day offshore tomorrow and everyone was psyched.

Now, standing on the dock at 5 a.m. Saturday morning, the wind whistles by ears at a solid 15 knots. Sometime between late last night and predawn, the weather changed. Listening to NOAA on VHF radio leaves a frown when your area's forecast comes on and declares wind all day.

The coolers are full with bait, ice, food, drinks, and the fuel tank is topped off. The crew is listening to the forecast as well and asks, giving that, are we going look? Sound familiar? Been there, done that? It is going to be an uncomfortable day of trolling, if not downright rough. Will it be worth it? Just might be! Often, the Fisherman has found a good bite on choppy days. Maybe the fish have to work harder for a meal and become more aggressive. But, if conditions are not dangerous, just uncomfortable, it might be worth biting the bullet to pound mile after mile offshore.

Fishing in rough water requires a few changes compared to fishing on decent days. The surface turbulence of rough/choppy water requires making a few changes to the spread. When the wind is blowing, tighten up the spread. This allows more lines to be fished in the wind without constant tangling. Also, a tight spread makes the best use of the boat's white water fish-attracting ability. Troll larger bait/lures that are visible in rough water. Skip baits that are difficult to see; use birds in front of rigged ballyhoo. Trolling spreader bars and daisy chains help produce additional commotion and draw attention to spread. Use heavier weight when rigging ballyhoo. They will spend more time underwater making them visible to fish. Lines tend to snap from riggers or flat line clips often. Assume it is a bite and immediately drop back. Choppy days are the ideal time to use a planner or down rigger and get bait deep. Fishing deep bait is good in any conditions, but excellent when Mother Nature is not cooperating.

Think safety first! Know the boat's limitations and never place the crew or self in danger to fish rough conditions. However, if a glutton for punishment, by adjusting to rough water techniques, the day can often be very productive.

When only seeing the tower from other boat, it is time to tighten up the spread.

These anglers found the yellowfin hungry when fishing on a "snotty" day.

Weather

Understanding weather is certainly advantageous before going through the inlet in less than perfect conditions. Old seaman swore they could tell weather by how bones felt. Maybe...who knows? They also went by conditions in the sky to help forecast.

Red sky in morning, sailor takes warning; red sky at night, sailor delight.

Mackerel sky and mares' tails make lofty ships carry low sails.

The higher the clouds, the better the weather.

A wind from the south has rain in its mouth.

Sea gull sitting on sand, a sign of rain at hand.

Can these sayings be used to predict weather? Doubtful. But, by watching weather maps with isobars and low pressure systems, one can get a pretty good handle on what conditions may be like. In a nutshell, when isobars are close together, don't bother sticking nose out the inlet; it is going to be windy. When a low pressure system approaches, the barometric pressure drops and the bite turns on! However, this low pressure system indicates bad weather is right over the horizon. The Fisherman tried to take advantage of a low pressure bite one time with thoughts that the day would be fishable, with a low predicted to arrive late in the evening. Murphy's Law prevailed; the low arrived eight hours ahead of schedule and seas quickly went from four-to-five feet to eight-to-twelve feet. The five-hour beating everyone and the boat took to get back to port was not worth the couple yellowfin caught. Venture forth in lousy weather with caution!!!

Tackled!

⚓ **TIGHTEN SPREAD**
⚓ **HEAVY BAIT**
⚓ **PLANER**
⚓ **BASICS OF WEATHER**

Chapter 39

BFF Club

Bottom fishing with friends and family

The Fisherman seldom had bottom fishing charter trips other than deep dropping. But there was no shortage of anglers consisting of family and friends ready to jump aboard for a day and become members of the Bottom Fishing Fun Club. Want just plain, old-fashioned, fishing fun? If so, this is the ticket where size and species are not nearly as important as catching smiles and laughs. Bay fishing provides a lot of this type of action. But for anglers who want to "ocean" fish, there is good news, since the boat does not need to venture far from the inlet. This makes the fishery ideal for a smaller craft and also allows first-time ocean anglers to see how they can handle swells and seasickness. Being able to see land wins half the battle over seasickness and allows an angler to get their sea legs!

Like all types of fishing, just dropping a line to the bottom does not make for success. It takes a little effort to find decent fishing. Any type of reefs found on charts or inshore structure is worth a shot. Most inlets have an artificial reef within a couple miles run, the perfect spot to target attention. Tackle can be kept at a bare minimum with spinning rods equipped with simple two hook bottom rigs. Keep hooks on the small side; size 4 is about right for the smaller species' mouths, like croaker or spot. Keep in mind small hooks can catch big fish, but large hooks leave anglers scratching their heads when bait is stolen. Sea bass, flounder, tautog, sea robins, and skates are common catches. And, of course, "sharks" are a kid's and adult's favorite and all can be caught on small hooks. If a hook is swallowed, just cut it off; do not try to remove. Many of the sharks will be dogfish with no teeth, but every now and then a spinner, dusky, or sand shark will find the hook. This either leaves the angler with a great story of having a reel spooled or hook bit off. If lucky, and hook catches corner of mouth, the angler just might land a trophy!

Even small sharks create a thrill for most anglers.

Bait

There is something magical about a tug on the end of a line indicating something is interested in what has been lowered down to the bottom. Kids and adults alike want to catch fish and, often, size is not an issue. Clams, bloodworms, and crab are excellent bait. But squid is a great all-around good, inexpensive bait. Everything in the ocean eats squid. Striping a squid down into hook-sized pieces is not difficult.

Regardless of size, squid of all sizes are cleaned and cut into hook-sized pieces in the same manner.

The first step is to remove the head by simply pulling it off.

The fins on the front of the squid are only on one side; lay squid down so the fins are on the bottom. Then cut mantel (body) open.

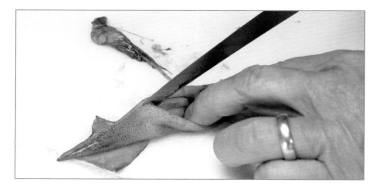

Next, remove inside of squid.

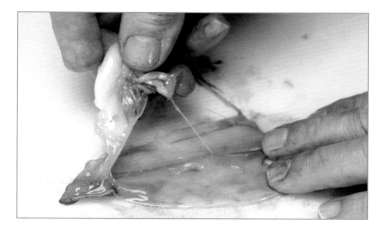

Turn squid over and, with knife blade, scrape off the skin.

Now, a clean white-looking piece of meat is left that only needs to be cut into hook-sized pieces. Cut bait tapering to points. To add additional bait movement, a slit can be cut from halfway down the piece of bait to the tip.

Probably the number one targeted bottom fish swimming in the ocean are sea bass. However, don't expect many keepers fishing inshore; they do keep smiles on a child's face, though. Chapter 31 covers sea bass in detail.

The popularity of Tog is growing. This is one species that does provide keepers inshore when water is cooler, mainly during spring, fall, and into winter.

However, during days of summer, once water warms, expect throwback Tog. Crab or sand crabs are excellent bait for these rod benders and structure fishing is required. Rock jetties lining access from bay to ocean is a great spot to begin the search. Chapter 17 goes into detail about these great-tasting fish.

A net should be onboard for those unexpected catches that occur from time to time. It is difficult to lift a four-pound flounder out of the water without falling off!

One species that keeps all anglers beaming are croaker. These tough little fighters are not picky eaters and as good in the frying pan as on the end of the line.

Bottom fishing may not have the allure of deep-blue water offshore, but for a family/friend outing, it is hard to beat the Bottom Fun Fishing Club.

Tackled !

⚓ **HOW TO CLEAN AND PREPARE SQUID FOR BAIT**

Chapter 40
Going Deep in the Deep

Deep dropping for golden tilefish

The Fisherman looked up from the conversation he was involved in at the Tiki Bar and noticed a good-sized crowd had gathered near the fish-cleaning station. Intrigued, he strolled over to find a captain he often fished with at the center of attention. Hanging on the scale was what was to become the new, world-record golden tilefish, also known as the great northern tilefish.

Since that day, when a thirty-year-old golden tilefish made the error of inhaling a tasty-looking squid, fishing strategy for many anglers changed. Only a handful of people from the marina deep dropped—actually a very small handful, as in the Captain who set the new world record and the Fisherman.

The popularity of deep dropping for golden tilefish and other species has grown by leaps and bounds since then. This is not a phenomenon only by anglers out of Ocean City, Maryland, but one for all along the East Coast. A fishery once specialized by mainly overnight head boats now has competition from charter boats targeting golden tilefish for clients. At the very least, charter boats fish for these beasts when trolling is less than productive. The savvy anglers may want to consider doing the same.

Catching golden tilefish is all about location, location, location. The fish are bottom dwellers found along the whole East Coast of the United States. They seem to favor 100-150 fathoms, where bottom temperatures remain constant in the low- to mid-fifties. The most important factor for locating fish is finding mud-type bottom. The fish create cone-shaped burrows on flat-to-sloped bottom and form small colonies; sand or rock prevents this from occurring. GPS coordinates are not found in books or when searching Google. Nor do anglers seldom give up numbers, unless handed down from generation to generation. This means it is up to the angler to find fish (which is very rewarding when it occurs). When seeking out bottom real estate to drop upon, try locating prime tilefish neighborhoods with the following advise.

Study canyons on the plotter and identify where there is a sharp drop off (contour lines close together) near the 100-fathom line. Then pick out a spot where, at the base of the drop off, the contour lines widen out in recommended depths, indicating bottom is changing to a slightly sloped or flat plateau. This is the ideal location to prospect. The fish do not feed 24/7, so it can be a time-consuming endeavor trying to identify where to drop lines. Certainly a lot of trial and error, with mostly error!

The Fisherman has sat right on proven numbers for close to two hours waiting for the bite to turn on, but when it finally did, all rods doubled over. Once fish are

The Fisherman (second from left),
along with family and friends,
are all smiles with this catch of
golden tilefish after spending the
day deep dropping.

Captain Ron Callis with his world-record
golden tilefish. Golden tilefish are easily
distinguishable from other members
of the family *Malacanthidae* by the
large adipose flap (crest on the head).
Sexual maturity is reached when fish
are approximately eight years of age,
twenty-seven inches, and weigh in the
neighborhood of nine pounds.

located, the numbers are golden, literally. Once taking up residence, fish do not migrate, except for small tiles that leave to establish new colonies or they risk being devoured.

Mark every fish caught on the plotter and, after time, an angler can tell the boundaries of the colony. Word of caution: a colony can be fished out, so think twice before sharing numbers. The pervious statement is not made with malice in mind. But the Fisherman made the mistake of giving GPS numbers for a newfound colony to "ONE" angler, who promised never to ever share the information. A couple weeks passed until the Fisherman decided to drop on the new colony again. As the boat approached the location, there were a half-dozen boats sitting right on the Fisherman's new numbers! Needless to say, no numbers were every shared with that individual again—not to mention the colony was fished out by the end of summer.

Equipment

A 4/0 or 6/0 reel matched to rod capable of handling two to four pounds of lead and spooled with a top shot of 300 yards of fifty- to eighty-pound test braid is all that's required to get started. For anglers who get serious about deep dropping, they will find the new lightweight jigging rods ideal for this fishery. These rods, with fast action tips, transfer pressure near the reel handle, easing lower back pain. This might be bottom fishing, but it is not easy. The lightness and balance of these outfits allow the rod to be worked all day with less fatigue. Stay away from stiff rods, like trolling outfits, if possible. High-speed reels, such as Shimano, Diawa, and Penn, all make reels that crank in over four feet of line per handle turn, making quick work when retrieving rigs off the bottom (if fifteen minutes of cranking to retrieve line is considered quick!). Braided line telegraphs bites to the surface; monofilament has too much stretch and creates drag in the water, requiring additional weight to hold bottom. Circle hook rigs are a must, since setting a J-hook is pretty much a fruitless attempt. Add enough weight to hold bottom and an angler is ready to go. Bait up, drop to bottom, and sit back and watch for rod to bend over!

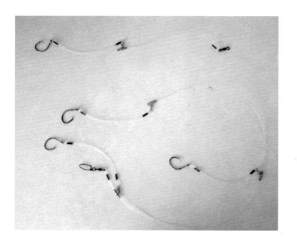

Deep drop rigs can be purchased or easily created. Typically, these rigs have four 10/0 to 13/0 circle hooks on six to ten inch drops. Create rigs using swivel sleeves for hook attachment on a piece of 150- to 200-pound leader material. Before crimping swivel sleeves, make sure they are spaced properly to prevent hooks from tangling. If looking for a world record, keep in mind there can be no more than two hooks on the rig.

Once becoming serious about deep dropping, anglers will want to melt lead and pour weights (saves $$$). Pick up a piece of one-inch-by-ten-foot conduit at a hardware store for seven bucks. Cut various lengths (four to eight inches) producing 1 to 2½-pound weights. When pouring, cover bottom with duct tape and stand pieces upright in dry sand. Pour lead and insert 3/0 barrel swivel in top immediately, before lead sets up for line

A buddy of the Fisherman is all smiles, and who wouldn't be with a golden tile like this one? When virgin colonies are found, they contain this size of fish.

attachment. Finish off by dipping weights when cool in can of Plasti-Dip ($7) to coat; this protects boat's gel coat! If lead is scrounged, for less than twenty bucks, a couple dozen weights can be made.

When wind or current creates drift in excess of 2 knots, bumping the boat in and out of gear allows lighter weight to be used and assists lines in remaining on bottom. This also allows the boat to stay on top of a colony for a longer period of time. Set up drift patterns, taking into account that lines fall into the abyss for more than a couple minutes before reaching bottom. It is easy to miss the "zone" with colonies the size of a football field. Tilefish are not picky eaters and find squid, clams, or fresh-cut fish appetizing. Electric reels certainly make life easy when retrieving 800 to 1,000 feet of line each drop. However, fish caught are not recognized for IGFA records.

Getting Jiggy

Anglers looking for more challenge than bottom fishing will be glad to hear tilefish are apparently sight feeders, even down in depths where very little light penetrates. It is either they can see or are attracted to the vibration of a jig bouncing up and down off the bottom. Either way, the Fisherman's crews have been using jigs with great success. Normally, the jigs' hooks are sweetened with squid, but many catches have been made on plain jigs.

Another benefit of using jigs is the ease that a line can be retrieved to surface without use of a heavy weight. Of course, chances of multiple hook-ups are lost. However, many anglers may find winding two forty-pound golden tiles up at a time just a bit more than they'd anticipated. Lightest jig the Fisherman has been able to reach bottom and work in 600 feet of water is a Shimano 9-ounce Butterfly—this on days with very little wind and current. Jigs in the one-pound range work better. Rig jig with one hook on top and one on bottom (see Chapter 31 for jig rigging options).

Danger! When that first tile comes over the transom, never reach bare hands under gills to lift fish for photo; gloves are a must to prevent cuts! This is not a catch-and -release fishery. After being cranked to the surface, the bladder is expanded and many times the fish is expired. On a rare occasion, when the hook pulls while winding up a tilefish, watch down current for a white floating belly. The expanded bladder prevents the fish from swimming back down to bottom and they float to the surface. Keep in mind by the time the fish reaches the surface, they are often a good distance from the boat (1/8 mile or more).

Next time your tuna/marlin day in blue water is not going as planned, try deep dropping. And while drifting, it's the perfect time to put a rod or two out with live bait for whatever pelagic is cruising around the area. Chapter 37 talks about kites; now is the time to utilize that strategy. Often, live bait opens up those locked jaws that were found when trolling.

The Fisherman smiles with approval as his nephew shows off a golden tile caught on a jig. The fish just missed the world record by a couple pounds.

Eating!

Author's Cream of Tilefish Delicacy

Similar to Cream of Crab, this recipe makes the run to the deep worthwhile!

Cream of Tilefish

Serves 6 to 8

Ingredients:

For Pre-Preparation
2 pounds golden tilefish filets
½ cup water
½ cup vinegar
2 tablespoons Old Bay seasoning

For Soup
1 stick butter
2 stalks celery, diced
½ gallon of Half & Half creamer
8 ounces cream cheese
8 ounces Velvetta processed cheese
2 tablespoons Old Bay seasoning
½ teaspoon nutmeg
1 tablespoon parsley
3 ounces cooking sherry

For Thickening Soup
2 tablespoons corn starch
1 cup milk, cold
Salt and pepper, to taste

Prior to Preparation:

Ahead of time, use double boiler with water and vinegar to steam tilefish filets with Old Bay seasoning until meat flakes easily with fork (approximately 10 minutes). Place in frig overnight. Next day, when cold, break into crab lump-sized pieces.

Directions:

In pot, melt butter over medium heat then add celery and continue cooking until celery is soft (3-4 minutes).

Add Half and half and continue cooking over medium heat while constantly stirring to prevent sticking. Once near boiling point, add remaining ingredients along with tilefish and turn heat to low and simmer for 20 minutes stirring occasionally to prevent sticking.

The final step is to turn the soup into creamy bisque. After simmering, stir two tablespoons of corn starch into a cup of cold milk. Turn heat back up to medium on soup bringing it to a soft boil. Add milk/corn starch, stirring constantly. Once thickened (10 minutes) add salt and pepper to taste.

Enjoy!!!

Tilefish has a lobster-like consistency. The broiled white meat dipped in butter satisfies the appetite of most lobster fans. For those who prefer crab, steam the meat until it flakes with a fork (do not overcook). Allow to cool, break into lump crab meat size and use to make mouth-watering crab cakes, crab imperial, or crab dip. Of course, broiling Tilefish with butter and garlic is another way to make an angler a fan of deep dropping!

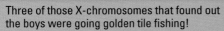
Three of those X-chromosomes that found out the boys were going golden tile fishing!

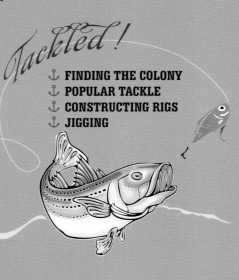

Tackled !

⚓ **FINDING THE COLONY**
⚓ **POPULAR TACKLE**
⚓ **CONSTRUCTING RIGS**
⚓ **JIGGING**

Chapter 41

Best Job?

So what better job could there be than chartering, getting to spend everyday offshore taking people fishing and getting paid for it? None, when looking at the surface of the job, but get down to the bottom and things become a little murky.

"Can you believe it? Went fishing and got paid for it!" The Fisherman's voice was ecstatic and he repeated the phrase over and over to anyone who made the mistake of answering the phone after his first "professional" day of mating. Several yellowfin were caught, the charter was happy, and the tip reflected all the effort he'd put forth. Years of fishing were finally paying off. Plus, even got paid to clean the boat! Yes Virginia, there is a Santa Claus.

Maintaining his personal boat and running offshore a couple times a week was putting a hurt on the Fisherman's wallet—not to mention the forty-hour week job that got in the way of fishing more. Fishing for a living had always seemed like the logical profession to pursue and now it had happened.

So how does an angler get this perfect job? In the Fisherman's case, it was right place, right time. Walking the docks one evening, he'd run into a captain cleaning up odds and ends in the dock box. The Fisherman had not seen him in a while and stopped to chat to find out how offshore fishing was going, plus, to try to pry loose a little catch information for the upcoming weekend. Conversation evolved into the captain mentioning being upset with the mate who didn't show up that morning. The snafu created an early-morning scramble to find someone who could fill in for the day.

And that fast it happened. "You interested in mating full time?"

If the Fisherman had never believed in God, he would have been converted that day. It took no longer to answer than time to form lips into the syllable: "Sure!" This occurred on a Wednesday; the next trips scheduled on the book were Friday and Saturday. A quick phone call and the old eight-to-four job was not in the way to prevent a dream from literally becoming reality, with new work hours from 4:30 a.m. to 8 p.m.

This occurred decades ago when regulations were relaxed concerning the chartering of boats. The coast guard required captains back then to obtain a six-pack license and there was a courtesy boat inspection; but, other than that, it boiled down to taking people fishing, catching fish, and getting paid. Most charter boats in the marina were booked several days a week. When bite was hot, working ten, fifteen, or even twenty days at a stretch was not uncommon when weather cooperated. There were plenty of charters to go around, a full day offshore was a manageable fee for six anglers at $500. Currently, it is a different industry

The Fisherman hard at work!

between insurances, inspections, and fees—not to mention licenses required to chase the various fish swimming in the ocean.

Is it worth it? For some yes, others no. Like any business, there are start-up costs before running that first trip offshore. Of course, boat and tackle can be depreciated along with a lot of tax write-off expenses. On the other side of the ledger is gross income. Good at catching fish? Better be, since the income side of ledger depends on that fact alone. Charter fees collected is the only source of income and in direct relationship to how successful the boat is when it comes to catching fish.

Every year, several boats left the marina that just didn't obtain enough charters to keep heads above water. Charter boats that catch fish, fish every day. Boats that don't, get overflow of anglers when bite is fast and furious with prime boats already booked. Otherwise, crews on second-tier boats sit, watching fish weighed, instead of weighing at day's end. Today, most marinas have more boats to go around than anglers. There's only so much public with pockets deep enough to shell out a couple grand or more for a day of offshore fishing. And this group shrinks each year with rising charter costs required to cover expenses. Add up cost of tackle, slip rental, fuel, insurance, mate, etc., and the boat better be running a lot of trips during the year if the owner/captain/mate expect to eat during the winter. Or income needs to be supplemented.

Anglers looking to get into chartering full time might be better off letting their boat sit and work a corporation boat for salary. Boats owned by businesses, or the one percent (as influential boat owners are apparently now called!), can afford tax write-offs without making profit. Being captain or mate on one of these boats provides steady paycheck with employment, even including health insurance. Unfortunately, there is a limited supply of jobs on million-dollar battlewagons. Experience is a perquisite along with references for these elite jobs. Single individuals or those married, looking to become divorced, are best suited for the job. The captain and mate are married to the boat, leaving little time to raise a family, let alone see them. Boat owners expect 100 percent dedication and going beyond job description when necessary, occurs often.

Not sure if that is the right deal? Then for the angler who owns a boat and works forty hours a week, just so he/she can breath in salt air on weekends, keeping a full time job and chartering part time on weekends might be in the cards. It also gives the opportunity to see if charter fishing really lies in the future. Chartering defrays the cost of owning a boat. As owner/captain, you will never get rich; actually, you will probably never make a cent. But this could work if you don't mind fishing with strangers on weekends who are willing to pay the freight, while you get to write off expenses. And when you get right down to it, does it get any better than fishing for free? Don't think so.

Oh yeah, if you are lucky enough to get a job as mate…show up!

Chapter 42

Catching Smiles

The boats docked at the end of the pier over the years always captured the attention and imagination of the Fisherman. His Dad owned several during childhood: runabouts, cabin cruisers, wood, fiberglass, outboards, and inboards. As a youngster, the vibration of a hull skipping over waves, combined with sun, wind, and spray in the face embedded boating deep in the soul. However, the most cherished memories certainly are of fishing.

The earliest recollection comes from around the age of six or seven years. Dad took the boat to a cove untouched by human ruin. He maneuvered into exactly the right spot and, ever so quietly, set the anchor. It was here, in the secret location that rods cast bait to a drop off just mere feet from shore where white perch cruised the shoreline for meals. The splendors of nature in this cove were everywhere eyes gazed. Various types of wildlife made appearances, moving stealthily out of woods, along with all types of birds nesting along the shoreline and up in trees. Egrets and herons in statue posture hid among reeds before demonstrating fishing skill second to none.

Boredom was never a problem waiting on a bite. Two minnows were suspended on a spreader rig beneath a red/white bobber. Tiny ripples of water radiated from the bobber caused from nervous minnows whenever a perch was close by. Anticipation of the bite was almost unbearable. Dad seized the opportunity to teach patience and insist that time be given for the fish "to take it." The thrill of hooking a fish when bobber submerged almost compared with the sound of "good job" or a pat on back that often followed when fish went on the stringer.

Over the years, Dad expanded fishing and learning to the Chesapeake Bay and Atlantic Ocean. Catching perch evolved into fishing for every species that roamed the mid-Atlantic.

Age has a way of sneaking up and stealing a childhood. Before long, the Fisherman was in the cove with his two young sons and shared the secret location. Dad often tagged along and both he and the Fisherman relished in the kids' squeals of delight when a bobber danced on the water.

The boys grew up with boat hulls under feet and fishing poles in hand. There were countless father/son fishing days over the years. There are no words for this bond and discussion about love of the sport is not necessary. Every treasured adventure will never be forgotten. The Fisherman's boys, now married with children of their own, are passing down the family's tradition and passion to the next generation's outstretched hands. Unfortunately, there's an empty seat in the boat as Dad passed twenty years ago. But carefully preserved memories in the back of the Fisherman's mind allow him to catch a smile fishing with Dad any time…along with a tear.

Wishing you all the happiness and joy in life that fishing has brought the Fisherman.

The author welcomes comments or questions and can be reached at SaltwaterTails@aol.com.

Acknowledgments

Over the years, there have been many people the author has shared a cockpit or helm, who unselfishly relinquished tricks of the trade. The following list is by no means complete and in no specific order. For everyone not included on the list and to all the anglers who have chartered with the author over time…a sincere **Thank You!**

Fred Unkart (Cuz)

Captain Ted Ohler

Lenny Rudow

Tom Kessler

Captain Josh Rusky

Tommy Rainer

Captain Ron Callis

Mate John Hardy

Captain Willie Zimmerman

Captain Ron Taylor

Mate Jon Meade

Mo Summerlin

And last, but certainly not least, my wife Marie and family who tolerate my passion for fishing.